THIS SEX WHICH IS NOT ONE

Also available in English
by the same author:
Speculum of the Other Woman

Luce Irigaray

THIS SEX WHICH IS NOT ONE

Translated by CATHERINE PORTER
with CAROLYN BURKE

CORNELL UNIVERSITY PRESS
Ithaca, New York

The publisher gratefully acknowledges the financial assistance of the French Ministry of Culture in defraying part of the cost of translation.

Originally published in French under the title *Ce Sexe qui n'en est pas un*,

First published 1985 by Cornell University Press.
Fourth printing, Cornell Paperbacks, 1988.

International Standard Book Number 0-8014-1546-2 (cloth)
International Standard Book Number 0-8014-9331-5 (paper)
Library of Congress Catalog Card Number 84-23013
Printed in the United States of America
Librarians: Library of Congress cataloging information appears on the last page of the book.

The paper in this book is acid-free and meets the guidelines for permanence and durability of the Committee on Production Guidelines for Book Longevity of the Council on Library Resources.

Contents

1. The Looking Glass, from the Other Side 9

2. This Sex Which Is Not One 23

3. Psychoanalytic Theory: Another Look 34

4. The Power of Discourse and the Subordination of the Feminine 68

5. Così Fan Tutti 86

6. The "Mechanics" of Fluids 106

7. Questions 119

8. Women on the Market 170

9. Commodities among Themselves 192

10. "Frenchwomen," Stop Trying 198

11. When Our Lips Speak Together 205

Publisher's Note and Notes on Selected Terms 219

THIS SEX WHICH IS NOT ONE

1

The Looking Glass, from the Other Side

> . . . she suddenly began again. "Then it really *has* happened, after all! And now, who am I? I *will* remember, if I can! I'm determined to do it!" But being determined didn't help her much, and all she could say, after a great deal of puzzling, was: "L, I *know* it begins with L."
>
> *Through the Looking-Glass*

Alice's eyes are blue. And red. *She opened them while going through the mirror. Except for that, she still seems to be exempt from violence. She lives alone, in her house. She prefers it that way, her mother says. She only goes out to play her role as mistress. Schoolmistress, naturally. Where unalterable facts are written down whatever the weather. In white and black, or black and white, depending on whether they're put on the blackboard or in the notebook. Without color changes, in any case. Those are saved for the times when Alice is alone.* Behind the screen of representation. *In the house or garden.*

But just when it's time for the story to begin, begin again, "it's autumn." That moment when things are still not completely congealed, dead. It ought to be seized so that something can happen. But everything is forgotten: the "measuring instruments," the "coat," the "case," and especially the "glasses." "How can anyone live without

This text was originally published as "Le miroir, de l'autre côté," in *Critique,* no. 309 (February 1973).

all that?" Up to now, that's what has controlled the limits of properties, *distinguished outside from inside, differentiated what was looked on with approval from what wasn't. Made it possible to appreciate, to recognize the value of everything. To fit in with it, as needed.*

There they are, all lost, without their familiar reference points. What's the difference between a friend and no friend? A virgin and a whore? Your wife and the woman you love? The one you desire and the one you make love with? One woman and another woman? The one who owns the house and the one who uses it for her pleasure, the one you meet there for pleasure? In which house and with which woman does—did—will love happen? And when is it time for love, anyway? Time for work? How can the stakes in love and work be sorted out? Does "surveying" have anything to do with desire, or not? Can pleasure be measured, bounded, triangulated, or not? Besides, "it's autumn," the colors are changing. Turning red. Though not for long.

No doubt this is the moment Alice ought to seize. Now is the time for her to come on stage herself. With her violet, violated eyes. Blue and red. *Eyes that recognize the right side, the wrong side, and the other side: the blur of deformation; the black or white of a loss of identity. Eyes always expecting appearances to alter, expecting that one will turn into the other, is already the other. But Alice is at school. She'll come back for tea, which she always takes by herself. At least that's what her mother claims. And she's the only one who seems to know who Alice is.*

So at four o'clock sharp, the surveyor goes into her house. And since a surveyor needs a pretext to go into someone's house, especially a lady's, he's carrying a basket of vegetables. From Lucien. Penetrating into "her" place under cover of somebody else's name, clothes, love. For the time being, *that doesn't seem to bother him. He opens the door, she's making a phone call. To her fiancé. Once again he slips in* between them, the two of them. *Into the breach that's bringing a woman and a man closer together, today at four o'clock. Since the relationship between Lucien and Alice lies in the zone of the "not yet." Or "never." Past and future both seem subject to quite a few risks. "That's what love is, maybe?" And his intervention cuts back across some other in-betweens: mother-Alice, Lucien-Gladys, Alice–her friend ("She already has a friend, one's enough"), tall-short (surveyors). To mention only what we've already seen.*

Does his intervention succeed? Or does he begin to harbor a vague suspicion that she is not simply herself? *He looks for a light. To hide his confusion, fill in the ambiguity. Distract her by smoking. She doesn't see the lighter, even though it's right in front of her; instead she calls him into* the first bedroom *where there must be a light. His familiarity with the house dispels the anxiety. He goes upstairs. She invites him to enjoy her, as he likes. They separate in the garden. One of them has forgotten "her" glasses by the telephone, the other "his" cap on the bed. The "light" has changed places.*

He goes back to the place where he works. She disappears into nature. *Is it Saturday or Sunday? Is it time for surveying or love? He's confused. There's only one thing to do: pick a fight with a "cop." The desire is compelling enough to make him leave at once.*

No more about cops, at least for the time being. He finds himself (they find each other) near the garden. A man in love and a man in love with a woman who lives in the house. The first asks the second, or rather the second asks the first, if he can go (back) and see the woman he loves. He is beginning to be frightened, and begs to be allowed . . . Afterward.

Good (common or proper) sense—any sense of propriety or property—*escapes Lucien. He gives things out, sets them in motion, without counting. Cap, vegetables, consent. Are they his? Do they belong to the others? To his wife? To somebody else's? As for what is his, it comes back to him in the* dance. *Which does not prevent him from allowing others to take it. Elsewhere.*

So he comes (back) in. It's teatime. She . . . She? She who? Who's she? She (is) an other . . . looking for a light. Where's a light? Upstairs, in the bedroom, the surveyor, the tall one, points out cheerfully. Pleased at last to come across a specific, unquestionable, verifiable fact. Pleased that he can prove it (himself) using a + b, *or 1 + 1, that is, an element that repeats itself, one that stays the same and yet produces a displacement in the sum; pleased that it's a matter of a series, of a sequence. In short, of a* story. *Might as well say it's* true. *That he had already been there. That he . . . ? That she? Was? Wasn't? She.*

For the vegetables no longer prove anything. "I must have eaten them." "I" who? Only the "light" is left. But it isn't there to shore up the argument. And even if it were, no trace of what has happened would remain. As for attesting that the light has moved from here to there, or stating that its current whereabouts are known, or naming Alice's room as the only place it can be found, these are all just claims that depend on "magic."

Alice has never liked occultism. Not that the implausible surprises her. She knows more than anyone about fabulous, fantastic, unbelievable things . . . But she's always seen what she talks about. She's observed all the marvels first-hand. She's been "in wonderland." She hasn't simply imagined, "intuited." Induced, perhaps? Moreover, from a distance. And across partitions? Going through the looking-glass, that's something else again.

Besides, there are no traces of such an adventure in that gentleman's eyes. It's a matter of nuances. So it's urgent for him to get out of the house at once. He won't? Then she's the one who'll leave, who'll desert it. The out-of-doors *is an extraordinary refuge. Especially in this season, with all its colors. He too goes into the garden. Right up close. So one no longer has the right to be alone? Where is one to go? If the house and garden are open to all comers. Omniscient surveyors, for example. It's imperative to hurry and invent a retreat they can't get to. Curl up somewhere protected from their scheming eyes, from their inquiries. From their penetration.* Where?

Lucien knows how to wait, even for quite a long time. His patience holds out indefinitely, at the edge of the vegetable garden. Installed outside the property, *he peels. Preferably beet stalks, which make little girls grow up. And lead them imperceptibly to marriage. From a long way off, very carefully, he's preparing a future. Improbable. That's not the only thing he's peeling. Perhaps that accounts for his arrival. Empty-handed. He doesn't even take the path, like everyone else. He comes across the grass. Always a little unseemly.*

Alice smiles. Lucien smiles. They smile at each other, complicitously. They are playing. *She makes him a gift of the cap. "What will Gladys say?" That he has accepted a gift from Alice? That she has offered him that cap? A "dragonfly" whose furtive flight volatizes the giver's identity in the present moment. Who deserves more gratitude, the woman who* duplicates *the possibility of sexual pleasure or the woman who offers it* a first time*? And if one goes back and forth between them, how can one keep on telling them apart? How can one know where one is, where one stands? The confusion suits Lucien. He's delighted. Since this is the way things are, since everyone is giving up being simply "myself," tearing down the fences of "mine," "yours," "his," "hers," he sheds all restraint. For although he looked as if he didn't care about anything, as if his prodigality were boundless, he was holding onto a little place for himself. A* hiding-place, *to be precise. A refuge, still private. For the day when everything goes wrong for everyone. For the time when troubles are too hard to bear. For a "rainy day." He's going to share that ultimate possession, that shred of property, with Alice. He's going to dissipate its private character. He takes her to a sort of* cave. *A concealed, hidden, protected place. A bit dark. Is this what Alice was trying to find? What he's looking for himself? And, since they've gotten to the point of telling secrets, they whisper in each other's ear. Just for fun, not to say anything. But Lucien realizes that the cap has been forgotten on the "bed." That detail disturbs his stability. Leads him to act hastily. In an echo effect, he'll slip up again. Very softly, whispering, in confidential tones, he nevertheless imposes what is.*

Is? *For him? For another? And who is he, to expose this way what might be? Alice is paralyzed. Closed up.* Frozen.

Since we've reached the point where we expound upon everyone's right to pleasure, let's go on to the lawyer's office. The meeting will take place outside. Inside, "the woman eavesdrops," he says.

"I've made love with a girl, in a girl's house. What am I in for?"

"Nothing." This outstrips anything one might imagine. All that for nothing. For free. Not even the shadow of a danger. Or penalty, or debt, or loss. Who can keep on surveying in the midst of such excesses? Yet there has to be a sequel. To the story.

Let's go on. "So I've slept with a lady I don't know, in the house of another lady I don't know. What am I in for?"

"Four years."

"Why?"

"Breaking and entering, cruelty. Two plus two make four, $2 \times 2 = 4$, $2^2 = 4$. *Four years."*

"How can I get off?"

"That depends on the two of them. Separately and together. First you have to identify these two non-units. Then go on to their relationships."

"I've identified one of them. The one to whom the coefficient 'house' can be assigned."

"Well?"

"I can't supply any other details, she's banned me from her property."

"That's too bad. And the other one? The vagabond, the wanderer: the mobile unit?"

"She's disappeared into nature."

"So . . ."

"Can you help me find her again?"

"My wife will be furious. I'll get dirty."

"I'll take you. I'll get you there. I'm the one who'll carry the load; I'll do the dirty work."

"O.K."

But where in nature? *It's huge. Here? There? You have to stop somewhere. And if you put his feet on the ground a bit too abruptly, of course he'll realize that he's covered with mud. Which was absolutely not supposed to happen. "What will my wife say?" What are we to think of a lawyer who gets his feet dirty? And* who, *after all, forbids dirtiness? The lawyer, or his wife? Why once again transfer to the other one the charge one refuses to address to one's own account? Because it might look a little disgusting. The gentleman's unattractive side. The one who claims he's a gentleman.*

Even though the surveyor came to get (back) on the right side of the law, he is revolted. If the numerical assessment gives him "four years," he sets the lawyer's worth at "zero." He's going to have to start over again from that point.

Lucien has gone back to Gladys's house. He's sighing. Again. Too much precision makes him sad. Lost. Indefinitely, he contemplates the representation of the scene, behind a windowpane. That unseen glass whose existence punctures *his gaze. Rivets it, holds it* fast. *Gladys closes the door of the house. Lucien speaks. Finally. "The scum, they've made love together." "Who's made love, Lucien? Who's one? Who's the other? And is she really the one you want her to be? The one you'd want?"* The ladies blur together, *virgin and/or whore. One blends into the other, imperceptibly.* Confusion *again becomes* legitimate. *The looking glass dissolves, already broken. Where are we? How far along? Everything is whirling. Everyone is dancing.*

Let's have some music, then, to accompany the rhythm, to carry it along. The orchestra is about to play. Somewhere else, of course. You've begun to notice that it is always in/on another stage *that things are brought to their conclusion. That the manifestation of things is saturated to the point where it exceeds plain evidence and certainty. Present visibility of the event. Incessant transferral: the complement of what is fomenting here moves over there—where? Moves from now to afterward—after the fact? From one to the other—who? And vice versa. Duplicating, doubling, dividing: of sequences, images, utter-*

ances, "subjects." Representation by the other of the projects of the one. Which he/she brings to light by displacing them. Irreducible expropriation of desire occasioned by its impression in/on the other. *Matrix and support of the possibility of its repetition and reproduction. Same, and other.*

The duet being (re)produced at the moment has Alice's mother and her fiancé as interpreters. The instruments—let us be clear—are cellos. For the first time the third party, one of the third parties, is a member of the party. Alice. Off to one side, in a corner of the room—a third bedroom—*she seems to be listening, or looking. But is she really there? Or is she at least half absent? Also observing what is going to happen. What has already happened.* Inside and outside. *Without presuming to know what might define either once and for all. Difference always in displacement. If "she" is dreaming, "I" must leave? The session continues. Someone has disappeared. Someone else is going to fill in for this missing subject. It's enough—just barely—to wait.*

He reopens the door of the house. Listens, looks. But his role is really to intervene. To subvert all the couples, by "stepping between." "Houses, people, feelings." In order to sort them out, possibly to reconcile them. After he has passed through, the surface has lost its other side. Perhaps its under side as well. But "how can anyone live without that?" With a single side, a single face, a single sense. On a single plane. Always on the same side of the looking glass. What is cut *cuts each one from its own other, which suddenly starts to look like any other. Oddly unknown. Adverse, ill-omened. Frigidly other.*

"How can anyone live with that?" "She's been cruel to me for five years!" "Just look at him: he always has a sinister look about him!" But when Eugene is imitating the cat whose tail has been cut off, when he unburdens himself, on the surveyor's person, of the only instrument whose intromission she allows into her house, he is fierce. And if she sighs, frets, weeps, you'll understand that she's not always cheerful. Moreover, just try to advise the one to leave since he is being made to

suffer; he'll leave his tool behind so he'll be sure to have to come back. Tell the other that she doesn't love him, not any longer: she'll laugh. Even if she's sad. And yet you were there—perhaps just for an instant—with eyes that know how to look, at least at a certain aspect of the situation: they can't find each other this time, they can no longer get back together. It's better for them to separate. At least for today. Anyway, they've never been united. *Each one has been putting up with the other's other. While waiting.*

Alice is alone. With the surveyor, the tall one. The one who made love with the one who took over her house. It even happened on her bed. She knows, now. He too has begun to understand the misunderstanding in the meantime. "Do you regret that mistake?" "No." "Do you want us to clear up the confusion?" ". . . ?" "Would you like to?" ". . . . . ?" How can they be differentiated in a single attribution?

How can I be distinguished from her? Only if I keep on pushing through to the other side, if I'm always beyond, *because on this side of the screen of their projections, on this* plane *of their representations, I can't live. I'm stuck, paralyzed by all those images, words, fantasies.* Frozen. *Transfixed, including by their admiration, their praises, what they call their "love." Listen to them all talking about Alice: my mother, Eugene, Lucien, Gladys . . . You've heard them dividing me up, in their own best interests. So either I don't have any "self," or else I have a multitude of "selves" appropriated by them, for them, according to their needs or desires. Yet this last one isn't saying what he wants—of me. I'm completely lost. In fact, I've always been lost, but I didn't feel it before. I was busy conforming to their wishes. But I was more than half absent. I was* on the other side. *Well, I can say this much about my identity: I have my father's name, Taillefer. I've always lived in this house. First with my father and my mother. He's dead now. Since then, I've lived here alone. My mother lives next door. And then? . . .*

"What did she do next?" She is not I. But I'd like to be "she" for you. Taking a detour by way of her, perhaps I'll discover at last what

"I" could be. "What did she do?" ?"She went upstairs to look for a light. She called me." "What's your name?" "Leon . . ." So I go up, since that's the way she's acted. The only thing I do differently—on purpose? by mistake?—is that I call his name from a different bedroom. The second. *He arrives, but it's the first room that he wants to go into. Is he mistaken again? Has he never been mistaken? For there to be a mistake, one of them has to be "she," the other not.* Is it possible to tell who is "she," or not? *What's important, no doubt, is that the scene is repeated. Almost the same way. From that point on,* "she" is unique. *However the situation may be re-dressed.*

"What do I do now?" "I don't know." Alice was all alone when she was elsewhere. When she saw all sorts of wonders. While she was coming and going from one side to the other. On this side, she is only acquainted with contrived points of reference, artificial constraints. Those of school, in a way: nursery school, grade school. And there, in front of him, she doesn't feel she is mistress. But he doesn't know that. Either. He takes off his coat, as she had done. And then? . . .

"First do I take off what I have on top, then underneath? Or the other way around? Do I go from outside to inside? Or vice versa?" ". . . ?" And because she has always been secretive, she has always hidden everything, and because in this hiding place no one has discovered her, she thinks it will suffice simply to turn everything inside out. To expose herself in her nakedness so that she can be looked at, touched, taken, by someone, by him.

"Do you like me?" Does he know? What does that mean? How can the source of pleasure be named? Why part with it for her? *And who, what is that "she" who is asking him,* scarcely a subject himself, *to assign her certain attributes, to grant her some distinctive characteristics? Apparently surveying isn't much use in love. At least not for loving her. How can anyone measure or define,* in truth, *what is kept* behind the plane of projections? *What goes beyond those/its limits? Still* proper *ones. No doubt he can take pleasure in what is produced there, in the person presented or represented. But how can he go beyond that horizon? How can he desire if he can't fix his line of sight? If he can't take aim at the other side of the looking glass?*

Outside, Alice, it's nighttime. You can't see a thing. You can't even walk straight, you can't stay upright, in the total darkness. You lose your balance. No more aplomb. At best, you're swaying. "Someone's limping outside. I'll go see."

The story *is coming to its end. Turning, and returning, in a closed space,* an enclosure *that is not to be violated, at least not while the story unfolds: the space of a few private properties. We are not going to cross a certain boundary line, we are not going above a certain peak. That would have forced us to find another style, a different procedure, for afterward. We would have needed,* at least, two *genres. And more. To bring them into articulation. Into conjunction. But at what moment?* In what place? *And won't this second one be just the* other side *of the first? Perhaps more often its complement. A more or less adequate complement, more or less apt to be joined by a copulative. We've never been dealing with more than one, after all. A unity divided in halves. More, or less. Identifiable, or not. Whose possibilities of pleasure have not even been exhausted. There are still remainders. Left* behind. *For another time.*

Because we're approaching the borders of its field, of its present frame, however, the affair is growing acrimonious. Subsequent events attest to an increasing exacerbation. But we can't be sure that it won't all end up in a sort of regression. With all parties retreating to their positions.

Since day has dawned, the surveyor, the tall one, *thinks it's fitting to take certain measures. Even if it's finally Sunday. Not daring to act alone, he phones the* short one *and asks him to go look for his coat, which he didn't forget at Alice's. To find out where things stand. To explain. To calculate the risks. Of an indictment . . . He takes him in his car up to the gate of the house. He's to wait for him in the bar, where he's meeting Lucien. Things are going rather badly between them. They've reached the point of insulting each other: "asshole" on the part of you know who, "rude" coming from the more timid one, who gets himself roundly scolded just the same for this insignificant outburst. It's because Leon doesn't joke around with rules; they're so necessary in his work. Alice doesn't have the coat, but she'll keep it. Because she wants to see him again. "Why do you want to?" "I just do." "Why?" "To live on the right side." But you can't understand what it's all about. You don't see anything at all. Or hardly anything. Well, it so happens that he has just noticed a detail that's crucial if we're to look the facts straight in the face: the glasses Ann forgot (?) by the telephone. She tries them on. Smiles. "How can anyone live without these?" They absolutely have to be given back to Leon, to whom they don't belong. Because everyone—and especially Leon and Alice—ought to wear them when something really important happens. It would help them straighten out the situation,* or the opposite. *Then they could throw them away. That's undoubtedly what Ann did. Little Max hands Ann's glasses over to Leon, while Alice is phoning her to tell her to come get them at her house, because she's afraid she'll break them: all glass is fragile in her hands. Leon uncovers the riddle of Ann's disappearance. She couldn't live without that. He goes to the police station and confesses everything. As for the policeman, he doesn't understand a thing.* Again, it's a question of optics. *He doesn't see any reason for severity, doesn't see the cause for guilt,* a fortiori *doesn't see the possibility of reparations. But he's ready to turn his job over to a specialist. So Leon is not allowed to clear himself. Increasingly overwhelmed, he goes back to her house, the house belonging to one of them, whom he now appoints as his judge. Ann got there on her bicycle before he did.*

Still looking for her, Alice gets Ann to tell how it happened. She reassures her, of course, that it was the same for her. And to prove (to herself) that she is really "her," Alice gets ahead of Ann in telling the rest of the story. She tells what happens when everything is already over. What happened to her the next day, which for her hasn't come yet. She says that love is fine once, but you mustn't ever start over again. Says that he may well be rather tiresome with his tendency to repeat everything.

Who spoke? In whose name? Filling in for her, it's not certain that she isn't trying also to replace her. To be even more (than) "she." *Hence the postscript that she adds to what was said to have taken place: "He even wants to have a baby with me." Then they fall silent, differently confused.*

That's the moment when the surveyor, of course, is going to intervene. But how can he tell them apart? *Who is she? And she? Since they are not the sum of two units, where can one pass between them?*

They get up, both of them, to answer him. But Ann can do it better. She's the one who'll tell him what they think. They? Or she? Which one? "One, or the other, or both of us, or neither." "It's you!" "It's I." She's right there in front of me, as if nothing had ever happened. So I've invented everything that was supposed to have happened to her? Everything she was? "I don't want to see you again." That's too much. Just when she is finally present again, when that seeing-again could finally be confirmed, perhaps, by recognition, she claims to disappear then and there. "And Alice?" "Not her either." Neither one nor the other. Neither one of the two. Nor the two, either, together or separately. How can she/they be allowed to escape that way? Behind. The door of the house, for example. "You cunt(s), you'll see me again, you'll hear from me. I'll come back with big machines and I'll knock everything down, I'll flatten everything, I'll destroy it all. The house, the garden. Everything."

Alice blinks her eyes. Slowly, several times. No doubt she's going to close them again. Reverse *them. But before her eyelids close, you'll have time to see that her eyes were* red.

And since it can't be simply a matter, here, of Michel Soutter's film,[1] *nor simply of something else—except that "she" never has a*

[1]"The Surveyors." The story goes like this: Alice lives alone in her childhood home, after her father's death. Her mother lives next door. Lucien and Gladys live in the same small village. There is also Ann, about whom we know nothing except that she makes love. And Eugene, Alice's friend, who only plays the cello. A highway is to cut through the village. So two surveyors arrive—Leon and Max. But surveying means "striding back and forth between houses, people, and feelings."

"proper" name, that "she" is at best "from wonderland," even if "she" has no right to a public existence except in the protective custody of the name of Mister X—then, so that she may be taken, or left, unnamed, forgotten without even having been identified, "i"—who?—will remain uncapitalized. Let's say:

"Alice" underground

2

This Sex Which Is Not One

Female sexuality has always been conceptualized on the basis of masculine parameters. Thus the opposition between "masculine" clitoral activity and "feminine" vaginal passivity, an opposition which Freud—and many others—saw as stages, or alternatives, in the development of a sexually "normal" woman, seems rather too clearly required by the practice of male sexuality. For the clitoris is conceived as a little penis pleasant to masturbate so long as castration anxiety does not exist (for the boy child), and the vagina is valued for the "lodging" it offers the male organ when the forbidden hand has to find a replacement for pleasure-giving.

In these terms, woman's erogenous zones never amount to anything but a clitoris-sex that is not comparable to the noble phallic organ, or a hole-envelope that serves to sheathe and massage the penis in intercourse: a non-sex, or a masculine organ turned back upon itself, self-embracing.

About woman and her pleasure, this view of the sexual relation has nothing to say. Her lot is that of "lack," "atrophy" (of the sexual organ), and "penis envy," the penis being the only sexual organ of recognized value. Thus she attempts by every means available to appropriate that organ for herself: through her somewhat servile love of the father-husband capable of giv-

This text was originally published as "Ce sexe qui n'en est pas un," in *Cahiers du Grif,* no. 5. English translation: "This Sex Which Is Not One," trans. Claudia Reeder, in *New French Feminisms,* ed. Elaine Marks and Isabelle de Courtivron (New York, 1981), pp. 99–106.

ing her one, through her desire for a child-penis, preferably a boy, through access to the cultural values still reserved by right to males alone and therefore always masculine, and so on. Woman lives her own desire only as the expectation that she may at last come to possess an equivalent of the male organ.

Yet all this appears quite foreign to her own pleasure, unless it remains within the dominant phallic economy. Thus, for example, woman's autoeroticism is very different from man's. In order to touch himself, man needs an instrument: his hand, a woman's body, language . . . And this self-caressing requires at least a minimum of activity. As for woman, she touches herself in and of herself without any need for mediation, and before there is any way to distinguish activity from passivity. Woman "touches herself" all the time, and moreover no one can forbid her to do so, for her genitals are formed of two lips in continuous contact. Thus, within herself, she is already two—but not divisible into one(s)—that caress each other.

This autoeroticism is disrupted by a violent break-in: the brutal separation of the two lips by a violating penis, an intrusion that distracts and deflects the woman from this "self-caressing" she needs if she is not to incur the disappearance of her own pleasure in sexual relations. If the vagina is to serve *also,* but *not only,* to take over for the little boy's hand in order to assure an articulation between autoeroticism and heteroeroticism in intercourse (the encounter with the totally other always signifying death), how, in the classic representation of sexuality, can the perpetuation of autoeroticism for woman be managed? Will woman not be left with the impossible alternative between a defensive virginity, fiercely turned in upon itself, and a body open to penetration that no longer knows, in this "hole" that constitutes its sex, the pleasure of its own touch? The more or less exclusive—and highly anxious—attention paid to erection in Western sexuality proves to what extent the imaginary that governs it is foreign to the feminine. For the most part, this sexuality offers nothing but imperatives dictated by male rivalry: the "strongest" being the one who has the best "hard-on," the longest, the biggest, the stiffest penis, or even the one who "pees the farthest" (as in little boys' contests). Or else one finds imperatives dictated by the enactment of sadomasochistic fantasies, these in turn governed by man's relation to his mother: the desire to force entry, to penetrate, to appropriate for himself the mystery of this womb where he has been conceived, the secret of his begetting, of his "origin." Desire/need, also to make blood flow again in order to revive a very old relationship—intrauterine, to be sure, but also prehistoric—to the maternal.

Woman, in this sexual imaginary, is only a more or less obliging prop for the enactment of man's fantasies. That she may find pleasure there in that role, by proxy, is possible, even certain. But such pleasure is above all a masochistic prostitution of her body to a desire that is not her own, and it leaves her in a familiar state of dependency upon man. Not knowing what she wants, ready for anything, even asking for more, so long as he will "take" her as his "object" when he seeks his own pleasure. Thus she will not say what she herself wants; moreover, she does not know, or no longer knows, what she wants. As Freud admits, the beginnings of the sexual life of a girl child are so "obscure," so "faded with time," that one would have to dig down very deep indeed to discover beneath the traces of this civilization, of this history, the vestiges of a more archaic civilization that might give some clue to woman's sexuality. That extremely ancient civilization would undoubtedly have a different alphabet, a different language . . . Woman's desire would not be expected to speak the same language as man's; woman's desire has doubtless been submerged by the logic that has dominated the West since the time of the Greeks.

Within this logic, the predominance of the visual, and of the discrimination and individualization of form, is particularly foreign to female eroticism. Woman takes pleasure more from touching than from looking, and her entry into a dominant scopic economy signifies, again, her consignment to passivity: she is to be the beautiful object of contemplation. While her body finds itself thus eroticized, and called to a double movement of exhibition and of chaste retreat in order to stimulate the drives of the "subject," her sexual organ represents *the horror of nothing to see.* A defect in this systematics of representation and desire. A "hole" in its scoptophilic lens. It is already evident in Greek statuary that this nothing-to-see has to be excluded, rejected, from such a scene of representation. Woman's genitals are simply absent, masked, sewn back up inside their "crack."

This organ which has nothing to show for itself also lacks a form of its own. And if woman takes pleasure precisely from this incompleteness of form which allows her organ to touch itself over and over again, indefinitely, by itself, that pleasure is denied by a civilization that privileges phallomorphism. The value granted to the only definable form excludes the one that is in play in female autoeroticism. The *one* of form, of the individual, of the (male) sexual organ, of the proper name, of the proper meaning . . . supplants, while separating and dividing, that contact of *at least two* (lips) which keeps woman in touch with herself, but without any possibility of distinguishing what is touching from what is touched.

Whence the mystery that woman represents in a culture claiming to count everything, to number everything by units, to inventory everything as individualities. *She is neither one nor two.* Rigorously speaking, she cannot be identified either as one person, or as two. She resists all adequate definition. Further, she has no "proper" name. And her sexual organ, which is not *one* organ, is counted as *none.* The negative, the underside, the reverse of the only visible and morphologically designatable organ (even if the passage from erection to detumescence does pose some problems): the penis.

But the "thickness" of that "form," the layering of its volume, its expansions and contractions and even the spacing of the moments in which it produces itself as form—all this the feminine keeps secret. Without knowing it. And if woman is asked to sustain, to revive, man's desire, the request neglects to spell out what it implies as to the value of her own desire. A desire of which she is not aware, moreover, at least not explicitly. But one whose force and continuity are capable of nurturing repeatedly and at length all the masquerades of "feminity" that are expected of her.

It is true that she still has the child, in relation to whom her appetite for touch, for contact, has free rein, unless it is already lost, alienated by the taboo against touching of a highly obsessive civilization. Otherwise her pleasure will find, in the child, compensations for and diversions from the frustrations that she too often encounters in sexual relations per se. Thus maternity fills the gaps in a repressed female sexuality. Perhaps man and woman no longer caress each other except through that mediation between them that the child—preferably a boy—represents? Man, identified with his son, rediscovers the pleasure of maternal fondling; woman touches herself again by caressing that part of her body: her baby-penis-clitoris.

What this entails for the amorous trio is well known. But the Oedipal interdiction seems to be a somewhat categorical and factitious law—although it does provide the means for perpetuating the authoritarian discourse of fathers—when it is promulgated in a culture in which sexual relations are impracticable because man's desire and woman's are strangers to each other. And in which the two desires have to try to meet through indirect means, whether the archaic one of a sense-relation to the mother's body, or the present one of active or passive extension of the law of the father. These are regressive emotional behaviors, exchanges of words too detached from the sexual arena not to constitute an exile with respect to it: "mother" and "father" dominate the interactions of the couple, but as social roles. The division of labor prevents them from making love. They produce or reproduce. Without quite knowing how to use their leisure. Such little as they have, such little indeed as they wish to have. For what are they to do with leisure? What substitute for amorous resource are they to invent? Still . . .

Perhaps it is time to return to that repressed entity, the female imaginary. So woman does not have a sex organ? She has at least two of them, but they are not identifiable as ones. Indeed, she has many more. Her sexuality, always at least double, goes even further: it is *plural*. Is this the way culture is seeking to characterize itself now? Is this the way texts write themselves/are written now? Without quite knowing what censorship they are evading? Indeed, woman's pleasure does not have to choose between clitoral activity and vaginal passivity, for example. The pleasure of the vaginal caress does not have to be substituted for that of the clitoral caress. They each contribute, irreplaceably, to woman's pleasure. Among other caresses . . . Fondling the breasts, touching the vulva, spreading the lips, stroking the posterior wall of the vagina, brushing against the mouth of the uterus, and so on. To evoke only a few of the most specifically female pleasures. Pleasures which are somewhat misunderstood in sexual difference as it is imagined—or not imagined, the other sex being only the indispensable complement to the only sex.

But *woman has sex organs more or less everywhere*. She finds pleasure almost anywhere. Even if we refrain from invoking the hystericization of her entire body, the geography of her pleasure is far more diversified, more multiple in its differences, more complex, more subtle, than is commonly imagined—in an imaginary rather too narrowly focused on sameness.

"She" is indefinitely other in herself. This is doubtless why she is said to be whimsical, incomprehensible, agitated, capricious

. . . not to mention her language, in which "she" sets off in all directions leaving "him" unable to discern the coherence of any meaning. Hers are contradictory words, somewhat mad from the standpoint of reason, inaudible for whoever listens to them with ready-made grids, with a fully elaborated code in hand. For in what she says, too, at least when she dares, woman is constantly touching herself. She steps ever so slightly aside from herself with a murmur, an exclamation, a whisper, a sentence left unfinished . . . When she returns, it is to set off again from elsewhere. From another point of pleasure, or of pain. One would have to listen with another ear, as if hearing *an "other meaning" always in the process of weaving itself, of embracing itself with words, but also of getting rid of words in order not to become fixed, congealed in them.* For if "she" says something, it is not, it is already no longer, identical with what she means. What she says is never identical with anything, moreover; rather, it is contiguous. *It touches (upon).* And when it strays too far from that proximity, she breaks off and starts over at "zero": her body-sex.

It is useless, then, to trap women in the exact definition of what they mean, to make them repeat (themselves) so that it will be clear; they are already elsewhere in that discursive machinery where you expected to surprise them. They have returned within themselves. Which must not be understood in the same way as within yourself. They do not have the interiority that you have, the one you perhaps suppose they have. Within themselves means *within the intimacy of that silent, multiple, diffuse touch.* And if you ask them insistently what they are thinking about, they can only reply: Nothing. Everything.

Thus what they desire is precisely nothing, and at the same time everything. Always something more and something else besides that *one*—sexual organ, for example—that you give them, attribute to them. Their desire is often interpreted, and feared, as a sort of insatiable hunger, a voracity that will swallow you whole. Whereas it really involves a different economy more than anything else, one that upsets the linearity of a project, undermines the goal-object of a desire, diffuses the polarization toward a single pleasure, disconcerts fidelity to a single discourse . . .

Must this multiplicity of female desire and female language be understood as shards, scattered remnants of a violated sexuality? A sexuality denied? The question has no simple answer. The rejection, the exclusion of a female imaginary certainly puts woman in the position of experiencing herself only fragmentarily, in the little-structured margins of a dominant ideology, as waste, or excess, what is left of a mirror invested by the (masculine) "subject" to reflect himself, to copy himself. Moreover, the role of "femininity" is prescribed by this masculine specula(riza)tion and corresponds scarcely at all to woman's desire, which may be recovered only in secret, in hiding, with anxiety and guilt.

But if the female imaginary were to deploy itself, if it could bring itself into play otherwise than as scraps, uncollected debris, would it represent itself, even so, in the form of *one* universe? Would it even be volume instead of surface? No. Not unless it were understood, yet again, as a privileging of the maternal over the feminine. Of a phallic maternal, at that. Closed in upon the jealous possession of its valued product. Rivaling man in his esteem for productive excess. In such a race for power, woman loses the uniqueness of her pleasure. By closing herself off as volume, she renounces the pleasure that she gets from the *nonsuture of her lips:* she is undoubtedly a mother, but a virgin mother; the role was assigned to her by mythologies long ago. Granting her a certain social power to the extent that she is reduced, with her own complicity, to sexual impotence.

(Re-)discovering herself, for a woman, thus could only signify the possibility of sacrificing no one of her pleasures to another, of identifying herself with none of them in particular, *of never being simply one.* A sort of expanding universe to which no limits could be fixed and which would not be incoherence nonetheless—nor that polymorphous perversion of the child in which the erogenous zones would lie waiting to be regrouped under the primacy of the phallus.

Woman always remains several, but she is kept from dispersion because the other is already within her and is autoerotically familiar to her. Which is not to say that she appropriates the other for herself, that she reduces it to her own property. Ownership and property are doubtless quite foreign to the feminine. At least sexually. But not *nearness.* Nearness so pronounced that it makes all discrimination of identity, and thus all forms of property, impossible. Woman derives pleasure from what is *so near that she cannot have it, nor have herself.* She herself enters into a ceaseless exchange of herself with the other without any possibility of identifying either. This puts into question all prevailing economies: their calculations are irremediably stymied by woman's pleasure, as it increases indefinitely from its passage in and through the other.

However, in order for woman to reach the place where she takes pleasure as woman, a long detour by way of the analysis of the various systems of oppression brought to bear upon her is assuredly necessary. And claiming to fall back on the single solution of pleasure risks making her miss the process of going back through a social practice that *her* enjoyment requires.

For woman is traditionally a use-value for man, an exchange value among men; in other words, a commodity. As such, she remains the guardian of material substance, whose price will be established, in terms of the standard of their work and of their need/desire, by "subjects": workers, merchants, consumers. Women are marked phallicly by their fathers, husbands, procurers. And this branding determines their value in sexual commerce. Woman is never anything but the locus of a more or less competitive exchange between two men, including the competition for the possession of mother earth.

How can this object of transaction claim a right to pleasure without removing her/itself from established commerce? With respect to other merchandise in the marketplace, how could this commodity maintain a relationship other than one of aggressive jealousy? How could material substance enjoy her/itself without provoking the consumer's anxiety over the disappearance of his nurturing ground? How could that exchange—which can in no way be defined in terms "proper" to woman's desire—appear as anything but a pure mirage, mere foolishness, all too readily obscured by a more sensible discourse and by a system of apparently more tangible values?

A woman's development, however radical it may seek to be, would thus not suffice to liberate woman's desire. And to date no political theory or political practice has resolved, or sufficiently taken into consideration, this historical problem, even though Marxism has proclaimed its importance. But women do not constitute, strictly speaking, a class, and their dispersion among several classes makes their political struggle complex, their demands sometimes contradictory.

There remains, however, the condition of underdevelopment arising from women's submission by and to a culture that oppresses them, uses them, makes of them a medium of exchange, with very little profit to them. Except in the quasi monopolies of masochistic pleasure, the domestic labor force, and reproduction. The powers of slaves? Which are not negligible powers, moreover. For where pleasure is concerned, the master is not necessarily well served. Thus to reverse the relation, especially in the economy of sexuality, does not seem a desirable objective.

But if women are to preserve and expand their autoeroticism, their homo-sexuality, might not the renunciation of heterosexual pleasure correspond once again to that disconnection from power that is traditionally theirs? Would it not involve a new prison, a new cloister, built of their own accord? For women to undertake tactical strikes, to keep themselves apart from men long enough to learn to defend their desire, especially through speech, to discover the love of other women while sheltered from men's imperious choices that put them in the position of rival commodities, to forge for themselves a social status that compels recognition, to earn their living in order to escape from the condition of prostitute . . . these are certainly indispensable stages in the escape from their proletarization on the exchange market. But if their aim were simply to reverse the order of things, even supposing this to be possible, history would repeat itself in the long run, would revert to sameness: to phallocratism. It would leave room neither for women's sexuality, nor for women's imaginary, nor for women's language to take (their) place.

3

Psychoanalytic Theory: Another Look

Freudian Theory

The Libidinal Organization of the Pre-Oedipal Phases

"Both sexes seem to pass through the early phases of libidinal development in the same manner. It might have been expected that in girls there would already have been some lag in aggressiveness in the sadistic-anal phase, but such is not the case. . . . With their entry into the phallic phase the differences between the sexes are completely eclipsed by their agreements. We are now obliged to recognize that *the little girl is a little man.* In boys, as we know, this phase is marked by the fact that they have learnt how to derive pleasurable sensations from their small penis and connect its excited state with their ideas of sexual intercourse. Little girls do the same thing with their still smaller *clitoris.* It seems that with them all their masturbatory acts are carried out on this *penis-equivalent,* and that the *truly feminine vagina* is *still undiscovered* by both sexes."[1] For Freud,

This text was originally published as "Retour sur la théorie psychanalytique," in *Encyclopédie médico-chirurgicale, gynécologie,* 3 (1973), 167 A-10.

[1]Sigmund Freud, "Femininity," in *New Introductory Lectures on Psycho-analysis, The Standard Edition of the Complete Psychological Works of Sigmund Freud,* ed. James Strachey, 24 vols. (London, 1953–1974), *22*:117–118; emphasis added. I shall make frequent use of this article since, written late in Freud's life, it reexamines a number of assertions developed in various other texts. All further quotations from Freud's writings, indicated by volume and page numbers, are from this edition.

the first phases of sexual development unfold in precisely the same way in boys and girls alike. This view finds its justification in the fact that the erogenous zones are the same and play a similar role: they are sources of excitement and of satisfaction of the so-called "component instincts." The mouth and the anus are the privileged erogenous zones, but the genital organs also come into play, for although they have not yet subordinated all the component instincts to the "sexual" or reproductive function, they themselves intervene as erogenous zones particularly in masturbation.

The primacy of the male organ

It does not seem to be a problem for Freud that the *mouth* and *anus* are "neutral" from the standpoint of sexual difference. As for the identity of the genital zones themselves, he draws upon biology and upon his own analytical observations to state that for the little girl *the clitoris alone is involved* at this period of her sexual development and that the clitoris can be considered a *truncated penis,* a "smaller" penis, an "embryological relic proving the bisexual nature of woman," "homologous to the masculine genital zone of the glans penis." The little girl is then indeed a little man, and all her sexual drives and pleasures, the masturbatory ones in particular, are in fact "masculine."

These assertions among others are developed in the "Three Essays on the Theory of Sexuality,"[2] in which it is asserted that the *hypothesis of a single identical genital apparatus—the male organ—is fundamental in order to account for the infantile sexual organization of both sexes.* Freud thus maintains with consistency that *the libido is always masculine,* whether it is manifested in males or females, whether the desired object is woman or man. This idea, relative both to the primacy of the penis and to the necessarily masculine character of the libido, presides, as we

[2]"Three Essays on the Theory of Sexuality," 7:125–243 (especially the third of these essays, in the 1915 version and later).

shall see, over the problematics of castration as developed by Freud. Before we reach that point, we must stop to consider some implications of this "beginning" of the process of becoming a woman.

Consequences for female infantile genitality

The little girl, according to Freud, does not lag behind the boy in terms of the energy of her component instincts. For example, "her aggressive impulses leave nothing to be desired in the way of abundance and violence" ("Femininity," p. 118); likewise, it has been possible to observe the "incredible phallic activity of the girl" (ibid., p. 130). Now in order for "femininity" to arise, a much greater repression of the aforementioned instincts will be required of the little girl, and, in particular, the transformation of her sexual "activity" into its opposite: "passivity." Thus the component instincts, in particular the sado-anal and also the scoptophilic ones, the most insistent of all, will ultimately be distributed in a harmonious complementarity: the tendency toward self-appropriation will find its complement in the desire to be possessed, the pleasure of causing suffering will be complemented by feminine masochism, the desire to see by "masks" and modesty that evoke the desire to exhibit oneself, and so on. The difference between the sexes ultimately cuts back through early childhood, dividing up functions and sexual roles: "maleness combines [the factors of] subject, activity, and possession of the penis; femaleness takes over [those of] object and passivity" and the castrated genital organ.[3] But this distribution, after the fact, of the component instincts is not inscribed in the sexual activity of early childhood, and Freud has little to say about the effects of the repression for/by women of this infantile sexual energy. He stresses, however, that femininity is characterized, and must be characterized, by an *earlier and*

[3]"The Infantile Genital Organization: An Interpolation into the Theory of Sexuality," *19*:145.

more inflexible repression of the sexual drives and a stronger tendency toward passivity.

In the final analysis, it is as a little man that the little girl loves her mother. The specific relation of the girl-woman to the mother-woman receives very little attention from Freud. And he turns back only belatedly to the girl's pre-Oedipal stage as a largely neglected field of investigation. But for a long time, and even at the last, *he considers the girl's desire for her mother to be a "masculine," "phallic" desire*. This accounts for the girl's necessary renunciation of the tie to her mother, and, moreover, for her "hatred" of her mother, when she discovers that in relation to the valued genital organ she herself is castrated, and that the same is true of every woman, her mother included.

The Pathology of the Component Instincts

Freud's analysis of the component instincts is elaborated in terms of the desires for anatomical transgression whose traumatizing repression he observes in neurosis, and whose realization he notes in cases of perversion: the oral and anal mucus zones are overcathected with respect to the genital zones; and by the same token, fantasies and sexual behavior of the sadomasochistic, voyeurist, and exhibitionist types are predominant. If Freud makes inferences as to the infantile sexuality of neurotics and perverts on the basis of their symptomatology, he indicates at the same time that these symptoms result either from a congenital disposition (here again we see the anatomical basis of his theory) or from arrested sexual development. Thus female sexuality could be disturbed either through an anatomical "error" ("hermaphroditic ovaries" determining a case of homosexuality, for example)[4] or else by arrested development at a particular moment in the process of becoming a woman:

[4]"The Psychogenesis of a Case of Homosexuality in a Woman," *18*:172.

thus the prevalence of the oral mucus areas that are found, also, in homosexuality. As for the scoptophilic and sadomasochistic instincts, they appear so significant that Freud does not exclude them from genital organization; he reexamines them in that context while differentiating them sexually—here we should recall the opposition between *seeing* and *being seen, causing to suffer* and *suffering*. It does not follow however that a sexual relationship resolved at this level would fail to be, in Freud's eyes, pathological. Feminine sexual pathology thus has to be interpreted, in pre-Oedipal terms, as a *fixation on the cathexis of the oral mucus region,* but also *on exhibitionism and masochism*. To be sure, other events may produce various forms of "regression," qualified as morbid, to the pregenital phases. In order to envisage such regressions, we shall have to retrace Freud's story of the "development of a normal woman," and more specifically the little girl's relation to the castration complex.

The Specificity of the Feminine Castration Complex

If the castration complex marks the decline of the Oedipus complex for the boy, the same is not true—the reverse is more or less true—for the girl. What does this mean? The boy's castration complex arises in the period when he observes that the penis or male member that he values so highly is not necessarily a part of the body, that certain people—his sister, his little playmates—do not have one. A chance glimpse of a girl's genital organs provides the occasion for such a discovery. If the boy's first reaction is to deny what he has seen, to attribute a penis, in spite of everything, to his sister, to every woman, and especially to his mother, if he wants to see, believes he sees the male organ in everyone no matter what the evidence suggests, this does not protect him from castration anxiety. For if the penis is lacking in certain individuals, it is because someone has cut it off. The penis was there in the beginning, and then it was taken away.

Why? It must have been to punish the child for some fault. This crime for which the penalty is the amputation of one's sex organ must be masturbation, a topic on which the boy has already received ample warnings and threats. We must not forget that masturbation is governed by a need for release of affects connected with the parents, and more especially the mother, whom the little boy would like to possess as the father does—we might say, "in the father's place." The fear of losing his penis, an organ with a very heavy narcissistic cathexis, is thus what brings the boy to abandon his Oedipal position: the desire to possess the mother and to supplant his rival, the father. Following upon this comes the formation of the superego, the legacy of the Oedipus complex and guardian of social, moral, cultural, and religious values. Freud insists on the fact that "*the significance of the castration complex can only be rightly appreciated if its origin in the phase of phallic primacy is also taken into account*" ("The Infantile Genital Organization," p. 144). For the phallus, as we have seen, is responsible for the regrouping and the hierarchization of the component instincts in infantile genitality. A single sex organ, the penis, is then recognized as valuable by girls as well as boys.

From this point on, one can imagine what the castration complex must be for the *girl*. She *thought she had, in her clitoris, a significant phallic organ*. And, like her brother, she got voluptuous sensations from it through masturbation. But the sight of the penis—and this is the inverse of what happens to the little boy discovering his sister's genitals—shows the girl to what extent her clitoris is unworthy of comparison to the boy's sex organ. She understands, finally, the prejudice—the anatomical prejudice—that is her fate, and forces herself to accept castration, not as the threat of a loss, the fear of a not yet accomplished act, but as a *fait accompli:* an amputation already performed. *She recognizes, or ought to recognize,* that compared to the boy she has no sex, or at least that *what she thought was a valuable sex organ is only a truncated penis.*

Penis Envy and the Onset of the Oedipus Complex

The girl child does not readily resign herself to this effective castration, which represents an irreducible narcissistic wound. This is the source of the "penis envy" which to a great extent determines her future development. Indeed, the girl child continues for a long time to hope that one day she will find herself endowed with a "true" penis, that her own tiny organ will yet develop and will be able to hold its own in a comparison with the one her brother has, or her playmates. While waiting for such hopes to be confirmed, *she turns her desires toward her father, wanting to obtain from him what she lacks:* the very precious male organ. This *"penis envy" leads her to turn away from her mother,* whom she blames for having so badly endowed her, sexually speaking, and whose fate, as she comes to realize, she herself shares: like her mother, she herself is castrated. Doubly deceived by her mother, her first "sexual" object, she abandons her *to enter into the Oedipus complex,* or the desire for her father. Thus the girl's Oedipus complex follows the castration complex, inverting the sequence observed for the boy.

But, *for the girl, this Oedipus complex may last a very long time.* For she need not fear the loss of a sex organ she does not have. And only repeated frustrations vis-à-vis her father will lead her, quite belatedly and often incompletely, to deflect her desire away from him. We may infer that, under such conditions, *the formation of the superego will be compromised,* and that this will leave the girl, the woman, in a state of infantile dependency with respect to the father, to the father-man (serving as superego), and making her unfit to share in the most highly valued social and cultural interests. Endowed with very little autonomy, the girl child will be even less capable of making the "objective" cathexes that are at stake in society, her behavior being motivated either by jealousy, spite, "penis envy," or by the fear of losing the love of her parents or their substitutes.

But even after she has transferred to her father her former

attachment to her mother, after completing this change in sexual "object" that her feminine condition requires, the girl child still has a long way to go. And, as Freud stresses, "the development of a little girl into a normal woman" requires transformations that are much more complicated and difficult than those required in the more linear development of male sexuality ("Femininity," p. 117). Indeed, if "penis envy" determines the girl's desire for her father, desired as the man who will perhaps give her one, that "desire," which is overly "active," still has to give way to the "passive" receptivity that is expected of woman's sexuality, and of her genitalia. The "penile" clitoral erogenous zone has to relinquish its importance in favor of the vagina, which "is now valued as the place of shelter for the penis; it enters into the heritage of the womb" ("The Infantile Genital Organization," p. 145). *The girl has to change not only her sexual object but also her erogenous zone.* This entails a "*move toward passivity*" that is absolutely indispensable to the advent of femininity.

The Desire to "Have" a Child

Nor is that all. The "sexual function," for Freud, is above all the reproductive function. It is as such that it brings all the instincts together and subjects them to the primacy of procreation. The woman has to be induced to privilege this "sexual function"; the capstone of her libidinal evolution must be the desire to give birth. In "penis envy" we find, once again, the motive force behind this progression.

The desire to obtain the penis from the father is replaced by the desire to have a child, this latter becoming, in an equivalence that Freud analyzes, *the penis substitute.* We must add here that the woman's happiness is complete only if the newborn child is a boy, bearer of the longed-for penis. In this way the woman is compensated, through the child she brings into the world, for the narcissistic humiliation inevitably associated with the feminine condition. To be sure, it is not by her father that the little girl will in reality have a child. She will have to wait until much later for this infantile desire to be achieved. And it is this refusal that the father opposes to all her desires that underlies the motif of the transfer of her drives onto another man, who will finally be a paternal substitute.

Becoming the *mother of a son,* the woman will be able to "transfer to her son all the ambition which she has been obliged to suppress in herself," and, as the lack of a penis loses none of its motivating power, "a mother is brought only unlimited satisfaction by her relation to a son; this is altogether the most perfect, the most free from ambivalence of all human relationships" ("Femininity," p. 133). *This perfect model of human love can henceforth be transferred to the husband:* "a marriage is not made secure until the wife has succeeded in making her husband her child as well" (ibid., pp. 133–34). The difficult course that the girl, the woman, must navigate to achieve her "femininity" thus finds its culmination in the birth and nurturing of a son. And, as a logical consequence, of the husband.

Post-Oedipal Pathological Formations

Of course this evolution is subject to *interruptions,* to periods of *stasis,* and even to *regressions,* at certain points. Such instances bring to light the pathological formations specific to female sexuality.

The masculinity complex and homosexuality

Thus the discovery of castration may lead, in the woman, to the development of "a powerful masculinity complex." "By this we mean that the girl refuses, as it were, to recognize the unwelcome fact and, defiantly rebellious, even exaggerates her previous masculinity, clings to her clitoridean activity, and takes refuge in an identification with her phallic mother or her father" (ibid., pp. 129–30). *The extreme consequence of this masculinity complex can be found in the sexual economy and in the object choice of the female homosexual,* who, having in most cases taken her father as "object," in conformity with the female Oedipus complex, then regresses to infantile masculinity owing to the inevitable disappointments that she has encountered in her dealings with her father. The desired object for her is from then on chosen according to the masculine mode, and "in her behavior towards her love-object" she consistently assumes "the masculine part." Not only does she choose "a feminine love-object," but she also adopts "a masculine attitude" toward that object. She changes, as it were, "into a man, and [takes] her mother in place of her father as the object of her love" ("The Psychogenesis of a Case of Homosexuality in a Woman," p. 154). We need not go to these extremes to find in the repeated alternation of masculinity and femininity as predominating forces a possible explanation for the enigma that woman represents for man, an enigma that is to be interpreted through *the importance of bisexuality* in the life of the woman.

Furthermore, the woman's masculine claims would never be entirely resolved, according to Freud, and "penis envy," seeking to temper her sexual inferiority, *would account for many of the peculiarities of an otherwise "normal" femininity.* For example: "a larger amount of narcissism" than the man has ("which also affects woman's choice of object"), "physical vanity," "little sense of justice," and even "shame," whose function would be primarily the "concealment of genital deficiency." As for "having less capacity for sublimating their instincts," and the corresponding lack of participation in social and cultural interests, we have seen that these deficiencies stemmed from the specific nature of the woman's relation to the Oedipus complex, and from the resultant effects on the formation of her superego. These characteristics of femininity, while not very heartening, to be sure, are nevertheless not pathological. They appear to belong, for Freud, to the "normal" evolution of femininity ("Femininity," pp. 133–34).

Frigidity

We might well be more disquieted by Freud's observation of the *frequency of sexual frigidity* in women. But, though he recognizes that he is dealing here with a phenomenon that is not yet well understood, Freud seems to want to see it as confirming the natural sexual disadvantage that he attributes to women. Indeed, "it is our impression that more constraint has been applied to the libido when it is pressed into the service of the feminine function, and that . . . Nature takes less careful account of its [that function's] demands than in the case of masculinity. And the reason for this may lie—thinking once again teleologically—in the fact that the accomplishment of the aim of biology has been entrusted to the aggressiveness of men and has been made to some extent independent of women's consent" (ibid., p. 131). The idea that frigidity might be the effect of such a conception—violent, violating—of sexual relations does not appear in Freud's analyses; there he attributes frigidity either to the sexual inferiority of all women, or else to some constitutional or even anatomical factor that disturbs the sexuality of certain women, except when he is admitting his own ignorance of what might account for it.

Masochism

As for *masochism,* is it to be considered a factor in "normal" femininity? Some of Freud's assertions tend in this direction. For example, the following: "the suppression of women's aggressiveness which is prescribed for them constitutionally and imposed on them socially favours the development of powerful masochistic impulses, which succeed, as we know, in binding erotically the destructive trends which have been diverted inwards. Thus masochism, as people say, is truly feminine" (ibid., p. 116). Or does masochism constitute a sexual deviation, a morbid process, that is particularly frequent in women? Freud would no doubt respond that even if masochism is a component of "normal" femininity, this latter cannot be simply reduced to masochism. The analysis of the fantasy "A child is being beaten"[5] gives a fairly complete description of women's genital organization and indicates at the same time how masochism is implied in that organization: the daughter's incestuous desire for her father, her longing to have his child, and the correlative wish to see the rival brother beaten, the brother who is detested as much because he is seen as the child that the daughter has not had with her father as because he is endowed with a penis, all these desires, longings, wishes of the little girl are subject to repression because of the taboo against incestuous relations as well as the one against sadistic, and more generally against "active," impulses. The result is a transformation of the desire that her brother be beaten into the fantasy of being herself beaten by her father, a fantasy in which the little girl's incestuous desires would find both regressive masochistic satisfaction and punishment. This fantasy might also be interpreted as follows: my father is beating me in the guise of the boy I wish I were; or else: I am being beaten because I am a girl, that is, inferior, sexually speaking; or, in other words: what is being beaten is my clitoris, that very small, too small male organ, that little boy who refuses to grow up.

Hysteria

Although hysteria gives rise to the inaugural scene of analysis and indeed to its discourse (see, in this connection, the *Studies on*

[5] "'A Child is Being Beaten': A Contribution to the Study of the Origin of Sexual Perversions," *17*:177–204.

Hysteria Freud published with J. Breuer), and although Freud's earliest patients are hysterics, an exhaustive analysis of the symptoms involved in hysteria and the establishment of their relation to the development of female sexuality would extend beyond the framework of this summary of Freudian positions; as it happens, moreover, no systematic regrouping of the various phases of the investigation of hysteria is to be found in Freud's work. Let us then simply recall that, for Freud, hysteria does not constitute an exclusively feminine pathology. In another context, the "Dora" analysis,[6] the modalities of the female Oedipus complex are defined in both positive and negative form, namely, the desire for the father and hatred of the mother on the one hand, the desire for the mother and hatred of the father on the other. This *inversion of the Oedipus complex* might be categorized within the symptomatology of hysteria.

Returning, belatedly, to the girl's pre-Oedipal phase, Freud states that in any event "this phase of attachment to the mother is especially intimately related to the aetiology of hysteria."[7] Even though hysteria exhibits Oedipal fantasies more than anything else—fantasies which, moreover, are often presented as traumatizing—*it is necessary to return to the pre-Oedipal phase* in order to achieve some understanding of what is hidden behind this upping of the Oedipal ante.

Return to the Girl's Pre-Oedipal Phase

Freud's reexamination of the issue of the girl's pre-Oedipal phase—which he was encouraged to undertake, and in which he was assisted, by the work of women psychoanalysts (Ruth Mack Brunswick, Jeanne Lampl de Groot, Helene Deutsch), who could serve better than he as maternal substitutes in the transference situation—led him to look more closely at this

[6]"Fragment of an Analysis of a Case of Hysteria," 7:3–122.
[7]"Female Sexuality," *21*:227.

phase of the girl child's fixation on her mother.[8] He ends up asserting that *the pre-Oedipal phase is more important for the girl than for the boy*. But in this first phase of female libidinal organization, he focuses particularly on certain *aspects* that might be qualified as negative, or at least as *problematic*. Thus the *girl's numerous grievances against her mother:* premature weaning, the failure to satisfy a limitless need for love, the obligation to share maternal love with brothers and sisters, the forbidding of masturbation subsequent to the excitation of the erogenous zones by the mother herself, and especially the fact of having been born a girl, that is, deprived of the phallic sexual organ. These grievances result in a considerable ambivalence in the girl's attachment to her mother; were the repression of this ambivalence to be removed, the conjugal relation would be disrupted by more or less insoluble conflicts. *The woman's tendency toward activity* is also understood, in large measure, as an attempt on the girl's part to rid herself of her need for her mother by doing what her mother does—aside from the fact that the little girl, as a phallic being, has already desired to seduce her mother and have a child by her. Overly "active" tendencies in the woman's libidinal organization thus often have to be explored as resurgences, insufficient repressions, of the relation to the mother, and the "instincts with a passive aim" are thought to develop in proportion to the girl's abandonment of her relation to her mother. Nor must we neglect the fact that the little girl's ambivalence toward her mother brings about *aggressive and sadistic impulses;* the inadequate repression of these drives, or their conversion into their opposites, may constitute the seeds of a later *paranoia* to be investigated both as stemming from the inevitable frustrations imposed by the mother on the daughter—at the time of weaning, or at the time of the discovery of woman's "castration," for example—and also from the little girl's aggressive reactions. This would account for the girl's fear of

[8]See "Female Sexuality" and "Femininity."

being killed by her mother, her mistrust, and her continuing preoccupation with threats emanating from the mother or mother-substitutes.

The "Dark Continent" of Psychoanalysis

Whatever may have been established in this area, Freud continues to qualify feminine sexuality as the "dark continent" of psychoanalysis. He insists that he has not gotten beyond the "prehistory of women" ("Femininity," p. 130), allowing in another connection that the pre-Oedipal period itself "comes to us as a surprise, like the discovery, in another field, of the Minoan-Mycenean civilization behind the civilization of Greece" ("Female Sexuality," p. 226). Whatever he may have said or written on the sexual development of women, that development remains quite enigmatic to him, and he makes no claim to have gotten to the bottom of it. In approaching it he advises caution, especially as regards the determining social factors that partially conceal what feminine sexuality might be. Indeed, these factors often place women in passive situations, requiring them to repress their aggressive instincts, thwarting them in the choice of objects of desire, and so on. In this field of investigation, prejudices threaten to impede the objectivity of research, and, seeking to demonstrate impartiality in debates that are so subject to controversy, Freud falls back on the affirmation that the libido is necessarily male, and maintains that there is in fact only one libido, but that in the case of femininity it may put itself in the service of "passive aims" (ibid., p. 240). So in no way does his account question the fact that this libido has to be more repressed in the sexual organization of the woman. This would explain the persistence, the permanence of "penis envy," even where femininity is most firmly established.

These appeals for caution, these modifications of earlier statements, do not keep Freud from neglecting the analysis of the determining socioeconomic and cultural factors that also govern the sexual development of women; nor do they prevent him from once again reacting—or continuing to react—negatively to the research of analysts who rebel against the exclusively masculine viewpoint that informs his own theory and that of certain of his disciples, male and female, where "the development of women" is concerned. Thus although he bestows his approval on the work of Jeanne Lampl de Groot, Ruth Mack Brunswick, Helene Deutsch, and even, with some reservations, Karl Abraham, and though he includes the results of their work in his latest writings on the problem, he still remains opposed to the efforts being made by Karen Horney, Melanie Klein, and Ernest Jones to construct hypotheses about female sexuality that are somewhat less predetermined by masculine parameters, somewhat less dominated by "penis envy."[9] No doubt in his eyes these efforts present not only the disagreeable situation in which he finds himself criticized by his students, but also the risk of calling into question the female castration complex as he has defined it.

Women Analysts Against the Freudian Point of View

Karen Horney

It was a woman, Karen Horney, who first refused to subscribe to Freud's point of view on female sexuality, and who maintained that the complex sequence of castration and the Oedipus complex, as Freud had set it forth in order to explain the sexual evolution of the girl child, had to be "reversed." This

[9] See "Female Sexuality" and "Femininity."

reversal significantly modifies the interpretation of woman's relation to her sex.

The "denial" of the vagina

Indeed, it is no longer "penis envy" which turns the girl away from her mother, who does not have one, and leads her to her father, who might give her one; rather *it is because the girl child is frustrated in her specifically feminine desire for incestuous relations with the father that she reaches the point, secondarily, of coveting the penis as a substitute for the father.* Thus the girl, the woman, no longer desires to be a man and to have the penis in order to be (like) a man. If she reaches the point of post-Oedipal longing to appropriate the penis for herself, it is to compensate for her disappointment at having been deprived of the penis-object—and/or to defend herself both against the guilt accruing to incestuous desires and against a future sadistic penetration by the father, which she fears as much as she desires it.[10] All this presupposes that *the girl has already discovered her vagina,* contrary to Freud's claims that the vagina remains unknown to both sexes for a long time.

For Horney it would not be appropriate to speak of the relation of the girl child to her vagina in terms of ignorance, but rather in terms of "denegation." This would account for the fact that the girl may appear not to know, consciously, what she knows. This "denegation" of the vagina by the little girl would be justified by the fact that knowledge of that part of her sex has not been sanctioned at this stage, and also by the fact that this knowledge is dreaded. The comparison of an adult male's penis with the child's diminutive vagina, the sight of menstrual blood, or perhaps the experience of a painful tearing

[10]Karen Horney, "On the Genesis of the Castration Complex in Women," in *Feminine Psychology: Papers,* ed. Harold Kelman (New York, 1967).

of the hymen during manual explorations may in fact have led the girl child to be afraid of having a vagina, and to deny what she already knows about its existence.[11]

The cultural neurosis of women

From this point on, Karen Horney set herself even further apart from the Freudian theses, in that she *appealed* almost exclusively *to determining sociocultural factors in order to account for the specific characteristics of the sexuality known as female.* The influence of American sociologists and anthropologists such as Abram Kardiner, Margaret Mead, and Ruth Benedict led Horney to distance herself more and more decisively from the classical psychoanalytic viewpoints, for which she substituted—or to which she joined while criticizing them—the analysis of social and cultural factors in the development of "normal" sexuality as well as in the etiology of neurosis. In this perspective, "penis envy" is no longer prescribed, nor inscribed, by/in some feminine "nature," a correlative of some "anatomical defect," and the like. Rather, it is to be interpreted as a *defensive symptom, protecting the woman from the political, economic, social, and cultural condition that is hers* at the same time that it prevents her from contributing effectively to the transformation of her allotted fate. "Penis envy" translates woman's resentment and jealousy at being deprived of the advantages, especially the sexual advantages, reserved for men alone: "autonomy," "freedom," "power," and so on; but it also expresses her resentment at having been largely excluded, as she has been for centuries, from political, social, and cultural responsibilities. *"Love" has been her only recourse,* and for that reason she has elevated it to the rank of sole and absolute value.

[11]Karen Horney, "The Denial of the Vagina," in *Feminine Psychology.* On this point, Horney reexamines and expands upon Josine Muller's position in "A Contribution to the Problem of Libidinal Development of the Genital Phase in Girls," in the *International Journal of Psychoanalysis, 13*:361–368.

Her "envy" would thus be the index of an "inferiority" that women share, in practical terms, with the other oppressed groups of Western culture—children, the insane, and so on. And her acceptance of a biological "destiny," of an "injustice" done her as regards the constitution of her genital organs, is tantamount to a refusal to take into consideration the factors that actually explain that so-called "inferiority." In other words, woman's neurosis, according to Karen Horney, would very closely resemble an indispensable component in the "development of a normal woman" according to Freud: she resigns herself to the role—which is among other things a sexual role—that Western civilization assigns her.[12]

Melanie Klein

The second woman who objected to Freud's theories on female sexuality was Melanie Klein. Like Karen Horney, she inverted, or "turned around," certain sequences of consecutive events that Freud had established. And, again like Horney, she argued that "penis envy" is a secondary reaction formation compensating for the difficulty that the girl, the woman, experiences in sustaining her own desire. But it was *through the exploration, the reconstruction, of the fantasy world of early childhood* that Melanie Klein challenged the Freudian system.

Precocious forms of the Oedipus complex

Her divergences from Freud are evident right away, as it were: from the "beginning." For Melanie Klein refuses to assimilate clitoral masturbation to masculine activity. The clitoris is a feminine genital organ; it is thus inappropriate to see it as

[12]Karen Horney, "The Overvaluation of Love," in *Feminine Psychology*. See also "The Problem of Feminine Masochism," "The Neurotic Need for Love," etc.

nothing but a "little" penis and to want the girl to find pleasure in caressing it on that basis alone. Moreover, *the privileged eroticization of the clitoris is already a process of defense against vaginal eroticization, which is more dangerous,* more problematic, at this stage of sexual development. Vaginal excitement occurs earlier, but the fantasies of incorporation of the father's penis and the destruction of the mother-rival that accompany it lead the girl to be anxious about countermeasures on her mother's part, for there is the risk that her mother, in seeking revenge, might deprive her of her internal sexual organs. Since no means of verification, no "reality" test allows the girl to determine whether these organs are intact, and thus to eliminate the anxiety resulting from such fantasies, she is led to a provisional renunciation of vaginal eroticization.[13]

In any event, the little girl does not wait for the "castration complex" before she turns toward her father. In Klein's view, *the "Oedipus complex" is at work in the economy of pregenital drives,* and especially the oral drives.[14] Thus not only does weaning from the "good breast" lead to hostility toward her mother on the girl's part—hostility that is projected onto the mother, in a first phase, causing her to be dreaded as a "bad mother"—but in addition this conflictual relation with the mother is aggravated by the fact that she represents the forbidding of the oral satisfaction of Oedipal desires, of that satisfaction which is opposed to the incorporation of the paternal penis. For Melanie Klein, the first form of the girl's desire for a penis is the desire to introject the father's. Thus it is not a matter of "penis envy" in the Freudian sense, not a tendency to appropriate to oneself the attribute of masculine power in order to be (like) a man, but rather the expression, as early as the oral phase, of feminine

[13]Melanie Klein, "Early Stages of the Oedipus Conflict," in *Contributions to Psycho-analysis, 1921–1945* (London, 1948).

[14]Melanie Klein, "Early Stages of the Oedipus Conflict and of Super-Ego Formation," in *The Psycho-analysis of Children,* trans. Alix Strachey (London, 1937).

desires for the intromission of the penis. The girl's Oedipus complex is thus not the counterpart of a "castration complex" that would induce her to hope to get from her father the sex organ she lacks; rather it is active from the time of the girl's earliest sexual appetites.[15] This Oedipal precocity would be accentuated owing to the fact that woman's genital drives, like the oral ones, privilege receptivity.

Defensive masculine identifications

Such Oedipal precocity no doubt has its dangers. The father's penis is capable of satisfying the little girl's desires, but it can also, and at the same time, destroy. It is "good" and "bad," life-giving and death-dealing, itself caught up in the implacable ambivalence between love and hate, in the duality of the life and death instincts. In addition, the first attraction for the father's penis has the father as its aim insofar as his organ has already been introjected by the mother. Thus the girl would take possession of the paternal penis, and potentially of the children, that are contained in the mother's body. This entails a certain aggressiveness toward the mother, who may then respond by destroying the "inside" of her daughter's body and the "good objects" already incorporated there. *The little girl's anxiety about both the father's penis and the mother's revenge usually obliges her to abandon this first, feminine structuration of her libido and to identify herself, in a defensive maneuver, with the father's penis or with the father himself.* She thus adopts a "masculine" position in reaction to the frustration, and the dangers, of her Oedipal desires. This *masculinity* is thus quite *secondary* and has the function of concealing—indeed of decisively repressing—incestuous fantasies: the desire to take the mother's place with respect to the father, and to have the father's child.[16]

[15]Melanie Klein, "The Effects of Early Anxiety-Situations on the Sexual Development of the Girl," in *The Psycho-analysis of Children.*

[16]Melanie Klein, "The Oedipus Complex in the Light of Early Anxieties," in *Contributions to Psycho-analysis.*

An Attempt at Reconciliation: Ernest Jones

Unlike Freud, Ernest Jones greeted with considerable interest the modifications that certain women such as Karen Horney and Melanie Klein brought to the earliest psychoanalytic theorizing about female sexuality. This was undoubtedly because Jones undertook *a much more thoroughgoing investigation of the "feminine" desires of men and the castration anxiety that accompanies the boy's identification with women's genitals, especially in his relation with his father.* Somewhat more cognizant of men's longing for and fear of such an identification, Ernest Jones was able to venture further in the exploration of the "dark continent" of femininity, and to hear in a less reticent fashion what certain women were trying to articulate as to their own sexual economy. It is also true he was less obliged than Freud to defend the foundations of a new theoretical edifice. Still, the fact is that, without acquiescing to the positions maintained by Karen Horney in the second part of her work, without breaking with Freud as some of his students, male and female, had done, Jones nevertheless attempted to reconcile the Freudian viewpoint and new psychoanalytic contributions concerning the sexual development of women, adding his own in the process.

Castration and Aphanisis

Casting himself more or less as an arbiter of the debate, and seeking to find potential agreement between divergent positions, Jones maintained the Freudian view of the female Oedipus complex but demonstrated that some discoveries about the girl's pre-Oedipal phase made by analysts working with children encouraged a modification of the way the relation between the girl and the Oedipus complex was formulated. To begin with, *Jones distinguishes castration*—or the threat of losing the capacity for genital sexual pleasure—*from aphanisis, which would represent the complete and permanent disappearance of all sexual pleasure.* Thinking along these lines makes it clear that the fear of "aphanisis," following upon the radical frustration of her Oedipal desires, is what induces the girl to renounce her femininity in order to identify herself with the sex that eludes her pleasure.[17] Thus she wards off, imaginarily, the anxiety of being deprived of all pleasure forever. This solution also has the advantage of appeasing the guilt connected with incestuous desires. If this option is carried to its logical conclusion, it leads to homosexuality, but it occurs in an attenuated form in the normal development of femininity. In the latter case, it represents a secondary and defensive reaction against the aphanisis anxiety that follows the father's nonresponse to the girl's desires.

Various Interpretations of "Penis Envy"

The little girl is already a "woman," then, before she passes through this reactional masculinity. And we find evidence of her precocious femininity in the so-called "pregenital" stages.[18] *Penis envy is first of all the desire to incorporate the penis within oneself,* that is, an allo-erotic desire already discernible in the oral stage. The centripetal zone of attraction of the penis is subsequently displaced owing to the operation of the *equivalence among mouth, anus, and vagina.* Taking this precocious desire for the father's sex into consideration, Jones is led to refine the notion of "penis envy." For him, what is at issue may be the girl's desire to incorporate or introject the penis in order to keep it "inside" the body and transform it into a child; or it may be the *desire to enjoy the penis during intercourse* (oral, anal, or genital); or, finally, it may be the *desire to possess a male organ in (the) place of the clitoris.*

[17]Ernest Jones, "The Early Development of Female Sexuality," in *Papers on Psycho-analysis,* 5th ed. (Boston, 1961).
[18]Ernest Jones, "Early Female Sexuality," in *Papers on Psycho-analysis.*

This latter interpretation is the one Freud prefers, thus accentuating the girl-woman's desires for masculinity and denying the specificity of her libidinal organization and her sex. Now the desire to possess a penis in the clitoral region would correspond above all to autoerotic desires, since the penis is more accessible, more visible, a better source of narcissistic gratification during masturbatory activity. The penis would be similarly favored in fantasies of urethral omnipotence, or in scoptophilic and exhibitionist drives. The pregenital activity of the girl child cannot be reduced to these activities or fantasies, and one might even argue that they develop only subsequent to her allo-erotic desires for the father's penis. It follows that, both in the so-called pre-Oedipal structuration and in the post-Oedipal phase, *"penis envy" in the girl is secondary, and often defensive, with respect to a specifically feminine desire to enjoy the penis.* The little girl has not, therefore, been from time immemorial a little boy, any more than the development of her sexuality is subtended by a longing to be a man. To wish that it were so would amount to an inappropriate suspension of the girl's sexual evolution—and the boy's as well—at a particularly critical stage of its development, the stage that Jones calls "deuterophallic,"[19] in which each of the two sexes is led to identify with the object of its desire, that is, with the opposite sex, in order to escape both from the threat of mutilation of the genital organ that emanates from the same-sex parent, the rival in the Oedipal economy, and also from the anxiety or "aphanisis" resulting from the suspension of incestuous desires.

Complements to Freudian Theory

We have already noted that such alterations of the theory are opposed by other women analysts, who support and develop

[19]Ernest Jones, "The Phallic Phase," in *Papers on Psycho-analysis.*

Freud's original views, and that in his later writings Freud himself draws upon their contributions to the study of the first stages of woman's sexual development.

Let us recall that Jeanne Lampl de Groot insists on the question of the *girl's negative Oedipus.* Before arriving at a "positive" desire for the father, which implies the advent of receptive "passivity," the girl wishes to possess the mother and supplant the father, and this wish operates in the "active" and/or "phallic" mode. The impossibility of satisfying such desires brings about a devaluation of the clitoris, which cannot stand up to comparison with the penis. The passage from the negative (active) phase to the positive (passive) phase of the Oedipus complex is thus achieved through the intervention of the castration complex.[20]

One of the characteristic features of Helene Deutsch's work is the accent she places on *masochism in the structuring of woman's genital sexuality.* In all phases of pregenital development, the clitoris is cathected to the same extent as a penis. The vagina is ignored, and will only be discovered in puberty. But although the clitoris (penis) may be assimilated to the breast or to the fecal column, its inferiority becomes obvious in the phallic stage, since the clitoris is much less capable than the penis of satisfying the active drives that have come into play. What becomes of the libidinal energy with which the devalued clitoris was once cathected? Helene Deutsch maintains that to a large extent this energy regresses and is reorganized along masochistic lines. The fantasy "I want to be castrated" takes over from unrealizable phallic desires. Such masochism, of course, must not be confused with the later "moral" masochism. It represents a *primary, erogenous, and biologically determined form of*

[20]Jeanne Lampl de Groot, "The Evolution of the Oedipus Complex in Women," in *The Psycho-analytical Reader,* ed. Robert Fliess (New York, 1948).

the masochism that is a constitutive element of female sexuality, a sexuality dominated by the triad *castration, rape,* and *childbirth,* to which is added, secondarily and as a correlative, the masochistic nature of women's sublimations, including those that enter into their maternal, nurturing behavior toward the child.[21]

After having recalled, following Freud's lead, that sexual development is governed by the play of three successive and yet not quite interchangeable oppositions—active vs. passive, phallic vs. castrated, masculine vs. feminine—Ruth Mack Brunswick focuses her analysis principally on the modalities and transformations of the activity/passivity dyad in the pre-Oedipal phase of female sexual development.[22]

For Marie Bonaparte, the singularity of woman's relation to libidinal life, her "disadvantaged" position, results from the fact that female genitals can be compared to male organs that have been inhibited in their growth owing to the development of "annexed" organs serving the purpose of maternity.[23] Beyond this, in her view, *three laws govern the sexual evolution of woman:* so far as the *object of desire* is concerned, all passive and active cathexes implied in the relation to the mother are transferred to the relation to the father; as for *instinct development,* the girl's sadistic fantasies will be transformed into masochistic ones during the passage from the "active" to the "passive" Oedipus; finally, the *privileged erogenous zone* is displaced from the clitoris (penis) to the "cloaca," then to the vagina, when clitoral masturbation is abandoned. For Marie Bonaparte,

[21]Helene Deutsch, *The Psychology of Women: A Psychoanalytical Interpretation,* 2 vols. (New York, 1945, 1944–1945; repr. 1967).

[22]Ruth Mack Brunswick, "The Preoedipal Phase of the Libido Development," in *The Psycho-analytical Reader.*

[23]Marie Bonaparte, "Passivité, masochisme et féminité," in *Psychanalyse et biologie* (Paris, 1952).

"cloacal" eroticism constitutes an intermediate stage between anal eroticism and the much later eroticization of the vagina. Thus the vagina is only an annex of the anus, or to be more precise it is not yet differentiated from it, and the cloacal opening as a whole is the dominant prephallic and postphallic erogenous zone, right up to the stage of postpubertal vaginal eroticization.[24]

The Symbolic Order: Jacques Lacan

Fifteen or twenty years after the controversies over female sexuality had cooled down, after the issues had been forgotten (repressed anew?), Jacques Lacan reopened the debate. He sought to stress, in particular, the fact that the questions had often been badly put, and also to draw up a balance sheet for those issues that, in his opinion, remained unresolved. Among these latter, he evoked new developments in physiology concerning the functional distinction between "chromosomic sex" and "hormonal sex," as well as research on "the libidinal advantage of the male hormone," which led him to reexamine the patterns according to which the "break" between the organic and the subjective occurs; he also brought back to our attention our continuing ignorance as to "the nature of the vaginal orgasm" and the exact role of the clitoris in the displacement of cathexes in erogenous zones and in "objects" of desire.[25]

The Phallus as Signifier of Desire

As for the divergent psychoanalytic opinions about female sexual development, Lacan *criticizes those points of view that dis-*

[24]Marie Bonaparte, *Female Sexuality,* trans. John Rodker (New York, 1953).

[25]Jacques Lacan, "Propos directifs pour un congrès sur la sexualité féminine," in *Ecrits* (Paris, 1966).

tance themselves from Freud's for neglecting the perspective of structural organization that the castration complex implies. An inadequate differentiation of the registers of the real, the imaginary, and the symbolic, and of their respective impacts in deprivation, frustration, and castration, for example, leads psychoanalysts to reduce the symbolic dimension—the real issue in castration—to a frustration of the oral type ("Propos directifs"). In order to delineate more sharply the symbolic articulation that castration has to effect, Lacan specifies that *what is at issue as potentially lacking in castration is not so much the penis*—a real organ—*as the phallus, or the signifier of desire.* And it is *in the mother* that castration must, first and foremost, be located by the child, if he is to exit from the imaginary orbit of maternal desire and be returned to the father, that is, to the possessor of the phallic emblem that makes the mother desire him and prefer him to the child.

Thus the operation of the symbolic order becomes possible, and the father's duty is to act as its guarantee. Thus he prohibits both mother and child from satisfying their desires, whether the mother identifies the child with the phallus that she lacks, or whether the child is assured of being the bearer of the phallus by satisfying, incestuously, the mother's desire. Depriving them of the fulfillment of their desire, of the "fullness" of pleasure, the father introduces them, or reintroduces them, to the exigencies of the symbolization of desire through language, that is, to the necessity that desire pass by way of a demand. *The ceaselessly recurring hiatus between demand and satisfaction of desire* maintains the function of the phallus as *the signifier of a lack* which assures and regulates the economy of libidinal exchanges in their double dimension of quest for love and of specifically sexual satisfaction.

To Be a Phallus or to Have One

"But one may, by reckoning only with the function of the phallus, set forth the structures that will govern the relations between the sexes. Let us say that these relations will turn around a '*to be*' and a '*to have*'. . . . Paradoxical as this formulation may seem, we shall say that it is in order to *be the phallus,* that is to say, the signifier of the desire of the Other, that a woman will reject an essential part of her femininity, namely, all her attributes in the masquerade. *It is for that which she is not*—that is, the phallus—*that she asks to be desired and simultaneously to be loved.* But she finds the signifier of her own desire in the body of the one—who is supposed to *have* it—to whom she addresses her demand for love. Perhaps it should not be forgotten that the organ that assumes this signifying function takes on the value of a fetish."[26]

This formulation of a dialectic of relations that are sexualized by the phallic function does not in any way contradict Lacan's maintenance of the girl's castration complex as defined by Freud (that is, her lack or nonpossession of a phallus) and her subsequent entry into the Oedipus complex—or her desire to obtain the phallus from the one who is supposed to have it, the father. Likewise, the importance of "penis envy" in the woman is not called into question but is further elaborated in its structural dimension.

"The Image of the Body": Françoise Dolto

Françoise Dolto's research on the sexual evolution of the little girl should also be cited.[27] She stresses the need for the mother to be recognized as "woman" by the father in order for the little girl to feel that her feminine sex has value; and she provides useful descriptions of the *structuration of the body image* at each

[26]Lacan, "The Signification of the Phallus," in *Ecrits: A Selection,* trans. Alan Sheridan (New York, 1977), pp. 289–290; emphasis and interpolated statements added. For an analysis of one of Lacan's more recent publications on female sexuality, see below, "Così Fan Tutti," Chapter 5.

[27]Françoise Dolto, "La libido génitale et son destin féminin," in *La psychanalyse,* no. 7 (Presses Universitaires Françaises).

stage of a girl's libidinal development, paying a great deal of attention to the *plurality of the erogenous zones* that are specifically feminine and to the corresponding *differentiation of the sexual pleasure of the woman.*

But, given the richness of her analyses and the pointedness of the questions raised in her study, we may regret that like most of the other protagonists in this debate over female sexuality she has not adequately attended to the historical determinants that prescribe the "development of a woman" as psychoanalysis conceives of it.

Questions about the Premises of Psychoanalytic Theory

To put certain questions to psychoanalysis, to challenge it in some way, is always to risk being misunderstood, and thus to encourage a *precritical* attitude toward analytic theory. And yet there are many areas in which this theory merits questioning, in which self-examination would be in order. One of these areas is female sexuality. If we reconsider the terms in which the debate has taken place within the field of psychoanalysis itself, we may ask the following questions, for example:

Why has the alternative between clitoral and vaginal pleasure played such a significant role? Why has the woman been expected to choose between the two, being labeled "masculine" if she stays with the former, "feminine" if she renounces the former and limits herself to the latter? Is this problematics really adequate to account for the evolution and the "flowering" of a woman's sexuality? Or is it informed by the *standardization* of this sexuality according to *masculine parameters* and/or by criteria that are valid—perhaps?—for determining whether autoeroticism or heteroeroticism prevails in man? In fact, a woman's erogenous zones are not the clitoris or the vagina, but the clitoris and the vagina, and the lips, and the vulva, and the mouth of the uterus, and the uterus itself, and the breasts . . . What might have been, ought to have been, astonishing is the *multiplicity of genital erogenous zones* (assuming that the qualifier "genital" is still required) in female sexuality.

Why would the libidinal structuring of the woman be decided, for the most part, before puberty—since at that stage, for Freud and many of his disciples, "the truly feminine vagina is still undiscovered" ("Femininity," p. 118)—unless it is because those feminine characteristics that are politically, economically, and culturally valorized are linked to maternity and mothering? Such a claim implies that everything, or almost everything, is settled as to woman's allotted sexual role, and especially as to the representations of that role that are suggested, or attributed, to her, even before the specific, socially sanctioned form of her intervention in the sexual economy is feasible, and before she has access to a unique, "properly feminine" pleasure. It is understandable that she only appears from then on as "lacking in," "deprived of," "covetous of," and so forth. In a word: castrated.

Why must the maternal function take precedence over the more specifically erotic function in woman? Why, once again, is she subjected, why does she subject herself, to a hierarchical choice even though the articulation of those two sexual roles has never been sufficiently elaborated? To be sure, this prescription has to be understood within an *economy and an ideology of (re)production,* but it is also, or still, the mark of a *subjection to man's desire,* for "even a marriage is not made secure until the wife has succeeded in making her husband her child as well and in acting as mother to him" (ibid., pp. 133–134). Which leads to the next question:

Why must woman's sexual evolution be "more difficult and more complicated" than man's? (Ibid., p. 117). And what is the end point of that evolution, except for her to become in some way her husband's mother? The vagina itself, "now valued [only] as a place of shelter for the penis . . . enters into the heritage of the womb" ("The Infantile Genital Organization," p. 145). In other words, does it go without saying that the little girl renounces her first object cathexes, the precociously cathected erogenous zones, in order to complete the itinerary that will enable her to satisfy man's lasting desire to make love with his mother, or an appropriate substitute? Why should a woman have to leave—and "hate" ("Femininity," pp. 121ff.)—her own mother, leave her own house, abandon her own family, renounce the name of her own mother and father, in order to take man's genealogical desires upon herself?

Why is the interpretation of female homosexuality, now as always, modeled on that of male homosexuality? The female homosexual is thought to act as a man in desiring a woman who is equivalent to the phallic mother and/or who has certain attributes that remind her of another man, for example her brother ("The Psychogenesis of a Case of Homosexuality in a Woman," p. 156). Why should the desire for likeness, for a female likeness, be forbidden to, or impossible for, the woman? Then again, *why are mother-daughter relations necessarily conceived in terms of "masculine" desire* and homosexuality? What is the purpose of this misreading, of this condemnation, of woman's relation to her own original desires, this nonelaboration of her relation to her own origins? To assure the *predominance of a single libido,* as the little girl finds herself obliged to repress her drives and her earliest cathexes. Her libido?

Which leads us to wonder *why the active/passive opposition remains so persistent in the controversies surrounding woman's sexuality*. Even though this opposition may be defined as characteristic of a pregenital stage, the anal stage, *it continues to leave its mark on the masculine/feminine difference*—which would draw from it its psychological tenor[28]—*just as it determines the respective roles of man and woman in procreation* ("Femininity"). What relation continues to maintain that passivity toward the anal-sadistic drives which are permitted to man and forbidden to—inhibited in—woman? What relation guarantees man sole and simultaneous ownership of the child (the product), the woman (the reproductive machine), and sex (the reproductive agent)? *Rape,* if possible resulting in *conception*—rape is depicted moreover by certain male and female psychoanalysts as the height of feminine pleasure[29]—has become the model for the sexual relation.

Why is woman so little suited for sublimation? Does she also remain *dependent upon a relationship with the paternal superego?* Why is woman's social role still largely "transcendent with respect to the order of the contract that work propagates? And, in particular, is it through its effect that the status of marriage is maintained in the decline of paternalism?"[30] These two questions converge perhaps in the fact that women are tied down to domestic tasks without being explicitly bound by any work contract: the marriage contract takes its place.

We have not exhausted the list of questions that psychoanalysis could raise as to the "destiny," in particular the sexual destiny, assigned to woman, a destiny too often ascribed to anatomy and biology—which are supposed to explain, among other things, the very high frequency of female frigidity.

But *the historical determinants of this destiny need to be investigated.* This implies that psychoanalysis needs to reconsider the very limits of its theoretical and practical field, needs to detour through an "interpretation" of the cultural background and the

[28]Freud, "Instincts and Their Vicissitudes," *14*:111–140.

[29]See Freud, "Femininity"; Helene Deutsch, *The Psychology of Women;* and Marie Bonaparte, *Female Sexuality.*

[30]Lacan, "Propos directifs."

economy, especially the political economy, that have marked it, without its knowledge. And psychoanalysis ought to wonder whether it is even possible to pursue a limited discussion of female sexuality so long as the status of woman in the general economy of the West has never been established. What role has been marked off for her in the *organization of property, the philosophical systems, the religious mythologies* that have dominated the West for centuries?

In this perspective, we might suspect the *phallus* (Phallus) of being the *contemporary figure of a god jealous of his prerogatives;* we might suspect it of claiming, on this basis, to be the ultimate meaning of all discourse, the standard of truth and propriety, in particular as regards sex, the signifier and/or the ultimate signified of all desire, in addition to continuing, as emblem and agent of the patriarchal system, to shore up the name of the father (Father).

4

The Power of Discourse and the Subordination of the Feminine

INTERVIEW

Why do you begin your book with a critique of Freud?

Strictly speaking, *Speculum*[1] has no beginning or end. The architectonics of the text, or texts, confounds the linearity of an outline, the teleology of discourse, within which there is no possible place for the "feminine," except the traditional place of the repressed, the censured.

Furthermore, by "beginning" with Freud and "ending" with Plato we are already going at history "backwards." But it is a reversal "within" which the question of the woman still cannot be articulated, so this reversal alone does not suffice. That is why, in the book's "middle" texts—*Speculum,* once again—the reversal seemingly disappears. For what is important is to disconcert the staging of representation according to *exclusively* "masculine" parameters, that is, according to a phallocratic order. It is not a matter of toppling that order so as to replace it—that amounts to the same thing in the end—but of disrupting and modifying it, starting from an "outside" that is exempt, in part, from phallocratic law.

This text was originally published as "Pouvoir du discours/subordination du féminin," in *Dialectiques,* no. 8 (1975).

[1] *Speculum de l'autre femme* (Paris, 1974).

But to come back to your question. *Why this critique of Freud?*

Because in the process of elaborating a theory of sexuality, Freud brought to light something that had been operative all along though it remained implicit, hidden, unknown: *the sexual indifference that underlies the truth of any science, the logic of every discourse.* This is readily apparent in the way Freud defines female sexuality. In fact, this sexuality is never defined with respect to any sex but the masculine. Freud does not see *two sexes* whose differences are articulated in the act of intercourse, and, more generally speaking, in the imaginary and symbolic processes that regulate the workings of a society and a culture. The "feminine" is always described in terms of deficiency or atrophy, as the other side of the sex that alone holds a monopoly on value: the male sex. Hence the all too well-known "penis envy." How can we accept the idea that woman's entire sexual development is governed by her lack of, and thus by her longing for, jealousy of, and demand for, the male organ? Does this mean that woman's sexual evolution can never be characterized with reference to the female sex itself? All Freud's statements describing feminine sexuality overlook the fact that the female sex might possibly have its own "specificity."

Must we go over this ground one more time? In the beginning, writes Freud, the little girl is nothing but a little boy; castration, for the girl, amounts to accepting the fact that she does not have a male organ; the girl turns away from her mother, "hates" her, because she observes that her mother doesn't have the valorizing organ the daughter once thought she had; this rejection of the mother is accompanied by the rejection of all women, herself included, and for the same reason; the girl then turns toward her father to try to get what neither she nor any woman has: the phallus; the desire to have a child, for a woman, signifies the desire to possess at last the equivalent of the penis; the relationship among women is governed either by rivalry for the possession of the "male organ" or, in homosexuality, by identification with the man; the interest that women may take in the affairs of society is dictated of course only by her longing to have powers equal to those of the male sex, and so on. Woman herself is never at issue in these statements: the feminine is defined as the necessary complement to the operation of male sexuality, and, more often, as a negative image that provides male sexuality with an unfailingly phallic self-representation.

Now Freud is describing an actual state of affairs. He does not invent female sexuality, nor male sexuality either for that matter. As a "man of science," he merely accounts for them. The problem is that he fails to investigate the historical factors governing the data with which he is dealing. And, for example, that he takes female sexuality as he sees it and accepts it as a *norm*. That he interprets women's sufferings, their symptoms, their dissatisfactions, in terms of their individual histories, without questioning the relationship of their "pathology" to a certain state of society, of culture. As a result, he generally ends up resubmitting women to the dominant discourse of the father, to the law of the father, while silencing their demands.

The fact that Freud himself is enmeshed in a power structure and an ideology of the patriarchal type leads, moreover, to some internal contradictions in his theory.

For example, woman, in order to correspond to man's desire, has to identify herself with his mother. This amounts to saying that the man becomes, as it were, his children's brother, since they have the same love object. How can the question of the Oedipus complex and its resolution be raised within such a configuration? And thus the question of sexual difference, which, according to Freud, is a corollary of the previous question?

Another "symptom" of the fact that Freud's discourse belongs to an unanalyzed tradition lies in his tendency to fall back upon anatomy as an irrefutable criterion of truth. But no science is ever perfected; science too has its history. And besides, scientific data may be interpreted in many different ways. However, no such considerations keep Freud from justifying male aggressive activity and female passivity in terms of anatomical-physiological imperatives, especially those of reproduction. We now know that the ovum is not as passive as Freud claims, and that it chooses a spermatozoon for itself to at least as great an extent as it is chosen. Try transposing this to the psychic and social register. Freud claims, too, that the penis derives its value from its status as reproductive organ. And yet the female genital organs, which participate just as much in reproduction and if anything are even more indispensable to it, nevertheless fail to derive the same narcissistic benefit from that status. The anatomical references Freud uses to justify the development of sexuality are almost all tied, moreover, to the issue of reproduction. What happens when the sexual function can be separated from the reproductive function (a hypothesis obviously given little consideration by Freud)?

But Freud needs this support from anatomy in order to justify a theoretical position especially in his description of woman's sexual development. "What can we do?" he writes in this connection, transposing Napoleon's phrase: "Anatomy is destiny." From this point on, in the name of that anatomical destiny, women are seen as less favored by nature from the point of view of libido; they are often frigid, nonaggressive, nonsadistic, nonpossessive, homosexual depending upon the degree to which their ovaries are hermaphroditic; they are outsiders where cultural values are concerned unless they participate in them through some sort of "mixed heredity," and so on. In short, they are deprived of the worth of their sex. The important thing, of course, is that no one should know who has deprived them, or why, and that "nature" be held accountable.

Does this critique of Freud go so far as to challenge psychoanalytic theory and practice?

Certainly not in order to return to a precritical attitude toward psychoanalysis, nor to claim that psychoanalysis has already exhausted its effectiveness. It is rather a matter of making explicit some implications of psychoanalysis that are inoperative at the moment. Saying that if Freudian theory indeed contributes what is needed to upset the philosophic order of discourse, the theory remains paradoxically subject to that discourse where the definition of sexual difference is concerned.

For example, Freud undermines a certain way of conceptualizing the "present," "presence," by stressing deferred action, overdetermination, the repetition compulsion, the death drive, and so on, or by indicating, in his theory or his practice, the impact of so-called unconscious mechanisms on the language of the "subject." But, himself a prisoner of a certain economy of the logos, he defines sexual difference by giving *a priori* value to Sameness, shoring up his demonstration by falling back upon time-honored devices such as analogy, comparison, symmetry, dichotomous oppositions, and so on. Heir to an "ideology" that he does not call into question, Freud asserts that the "masculine" is the sexual model, that no representation of desire can fail to take it as the standard, can fail to submit to it. In so doing, Freud makes manifest the presuppositions of the scene of representation: *the sexual indifference* that subtends it assures its coherence and its closure. Indirectly, then, he suggests how it might be analyzed. But he never carries out the potential articulation between the organization of the unconscious and the difference between the sexes. —Which is a theoretical and practical deficiency that may in turn constrict the scene of the unconscious. Or might it rather serve as the *interpretive lever* for its unfolding?

Thus we might wonder whether certain properties attributed to the unconscious may not, in part, be ascribed to the female sex, which is censured by the logic of consciousness. Whether the feminine *has* an unconscious or whether it *is* the unconscious. And so forth. Leaving these questions unanswered means that psychoanalyzing a woman is tantamount to adapting her to a society of a masculine type.

And of course it would be interesting to know what might become of psychoanalytic notions in a culture that did not repress the feminine. Since the recognition of a "specific" female sexuality would challenge the monopoly on value held by the masculine sex alone, in the final analysis by the father, what meaning could the Oedipus complex have in a symbolic system other than patriarchy?

But that order is indeed the one that lays down the law today. To fail to recognize this would be as naive as to let it continue to rule without questioning the conditions that make its domination possible. So the fact that Freud—or psychoanalytic theory in general—takes sexuality as a theme, as a discursive object, has not led to an interpretation of the *sexualization of discourse* itself, certainly not to an interpretation of Freud's own discourse. His resolutely "masculine" viewpoint on female sexuality attests to this as well as his very selective attention to the theoretical contributions of female analysts. Where sexual difference is in question, Freud does not fully analyze the presuppositions of the production of discourse. In other words, the questions that Freud's theory and practice address to the scene of representation do not include the question of the sexualized determination of that scene. Because it lacks that articulation, Freud's contribution remains, in part—and precisely where the difference between the sexes is concerned—caught up in metaphysical presuppositions.

All of which has led you to an interpretive rereading of the texts that define the history of philosophy?

Yes, for unless we limit ourselves naively—or perhaps strategically—to some kind of limited or marginal issue, it is indeed precisely philosophical discourse that we have to challenge, and *disrupt,* inasmuch as this discourse sets forth the law for all others, inasmuch as it constitutes the discourse on discourse.

Thus we have had to go back to it in order to try to find out what accounts for the power of its systematicity, the force of its cohesion, the resourcefulness of its strategies, the general applicability of its law and its value. That is, its *position of mastery,* and of potential reappropriation of the various productions of history.

Now, this domination of the philosophic logos stems in large part from its power to *reduce all others to the economy of the Same.* The teleologically constructive project it takes on is always also a project of diversion, deflection, reduction of the other in the Same. And, in its greatest generality perhaps, from its power to *eradicate the difference between the sexes* in systems that are self-representative of a "masculine subject."

Whence the necessity of "reopening" the figures of philosophical discourse—idea, substance, subject, transcendental subjectivity, absolute knowledge—in order to pry out of them what they have borrowed that is feminine, from the feminine, to make them "render up" and give back what they owe the feminine. This may be done in various ways, along various "paths"; moreover, at minimum several of these must be pursued.

One way is to interrogate *the conditions under which systematicity itself is possible:* what the coherence of the discursive utterance conceals of the conditions under which it is produced, whatever it may say about these conditions in discourse. For example the "matter" from which the speaking subject draws nourishment in order to produce itself, to reproduce itself; the *scenography* that makes representation feasible, representation as defined in philosophy, that is, the architectonics of its theatre, its framing in space-time, its geometric organization, its props, its actors, their respective positions, their dialogues, indeed their tragic relations, without overlooking the *mirror,* most often hidden, that allows the logos, the subject, to reduplicate itself, to reflect itself by itself. All these are interventions on the scene; they ensure its coherence so long as they remain uninterpreted. Thus they have to be reenacted, in each figure of discourse, in order to shake discourse away from its mooring in the value of "presence." For each philosopher, beginning with those whose names define some age in the history of philosophy, we have to point out how the break with material contiguity is made, how the system is put together, how the specular economy works.

This process of interpretive rereading has always been a *psychoanalytic undertaking* as well. That is why we need to pay attention to the way the unconscious works in each philosophy, and perhaps in philosophy in general. We need to listen (psycho)analytically to its procedures of repression, to the structuration of language that shores up its representations, separating the true from the false, the meaningful from the meaningless, and so forth. This does not mean that we have to give ourselves over to some kind of symbolic, point-by-point interpretation of philosophers' utterances. Moreover, even if we were to do so, we would still be leaving the mystery of "the origin" intact. What is called for instead is an examination of the *operation of the "grammar"* of each figure of discourse, its syntactic laws or requirements, its imaginary configurations, its metaphoric networks, and also, of course, what it does not articulate at the level of utterance: *its silences.*

But as we have already seen, even with the help of linguistics, psychoanalysis cannot solve the problem of the articulation of the female sex in discourse. Even though Freud's theory, through an effect of dress-rehearsal—at least as far as the relation between the sexes is concerned—shows clearly the function of the feminine in that scene. *What remains to be done, then, is to work at "destroying" the discursive mechanism.* Which is not a simple undertaking . . . For how can we introduce ourselves into such a tightly-woven systematicity?

There is, in an initial phase, perhaps only one "path," the one historically assigned to the feminine: that of *mimicry*. One must assume the feminine role deliberately. Which means already to convert a form of subordination into an affirmation, and thus to begin to thwart it. Whereas a direct feminine challenge to this condition means demanding to speak as a (masculine) "subject," that is, it means to postulate a relation to the intelligible that would maintain sexual indifference.

To play with mimesis is thus, for a woman, to try to recover the place of her exploitation by discourse, without allowing herself to be simply reduced to it. It means to resubmit herself—inasmuch as she is on the side of the "perceptible," of "matter"—to "ideas," in particular to ideas about herself, that are elaborated in/by a masculine logic, but so as to make "visible," by an effect of playful repetition, what was supposed to remain invisible: the cover-up of a possible operation of the feminine in language. It also means "to unveil" the fact that, if women are such good mimics, it is because they are not simply resorbed in this function. *They also remain elsewhere:* another case of the persistence of "matter," but also of "sexual pleasure."

Elsewhere of "matter": if women can play with mimesis, it is because they are capable of bringing new nourishment to its operation. Because they have always nourished this operation?

Is not the "first" stake in mimesis that of re-producing (from) nature? Of giving it form in order to appropriate it for oneself? As guardians of "nature," are not women the ones who maintain, thus who make possible, the resource of mimesis for men? For the logos?

It is here, of course, that the hypothesis of a reversal—within the phallic order—is always possible. Re-semblance cannot do without red blood. Mother-matter-nature must go on forever nourishing speculation. But this re-source is also rejected as the waste product of reflection, cast outside as what resists it: as madness. Besides the ambivalence that the nourishing phallic mother attracts to herself, this function leaves woman's sexual pleasure aside.

That *"elsewhere" of female pleasure* might rather be sought first in the place where it sustains ek-stasy in the transcendental. The place where it serves as security for a narcissism extrapolated into the "God" of men. It can play this role only at the price of its ultimate withdrawal from prospection, of its "virginity" unsuited for the representation of self. Feminine pleasure has to remain inarticulate in language, in its own language, if it is not to threaten the underpinnings of logical operations. And so what is most strictly forbidden to women today is that they should attempt to express their own pleasure.

That "elsewhere" of feminine pleasure can be found only at the price of *crossing back through the mirror that subtends all speculation.* For this pleasure is not simply situated in a process of reflection or mimesis, nor on one side of this process or the other: neither on the near side, the empirical realm that is opaque to all language, nor on the far side, the self-sufficient infinite of the God of men. Instead, it refers all these categories and ruptures back to the necessities of the self-representation of phallic desire in discourse. A playful crossing, and an unsettling one, which would allow woman to rediscover the place of her "self-affection." Of her "god," we might say. A god to which one can obviously not have recourse—unless its *duality* is granted—without leading the feminine right back into the phallocratic economy.

Does this retraversal of discourse in order to rediscover a "feminine" place suppose a certain work on/of language?

It is surely not a matter of interpreting the operation of discourse while remaining within the same type of utterance as the one that guarantees discursive coherence. This is moreover the danger of every statement, every discussion, *about Speculum*. And, more generally speaking, of every discussion *about* the question of woman. For to speak *of* or *about* woman may always boil down to, or be understood as, a recuperation of the feminine within a logic that maintains it in repression, censorship, nonrecognition.

In other words, the issue is not one of elaborating a new theory of which woman would be the *subject* or the *object,* but of jamming the theoretical machinery itself, of suspending its pretension to the production of a truth and of a meaning that are excessively univocal. Which presupposes that women do not aspire simply to be men's equals in knowledge. That they do not claim to be rivaling men in constructing a logic of the feminine that would still take onto-theo-logic as its model, but that they are rather attempting to wrest this question away from the ecomony of the logos. They should not put it, then, in the form "What is woman?" but rather, repeating/interpreting the way in which, within discourse, the feminine finds itself defined as lack, deficiency, or as imitation and negative image of the subject, they should signify that with respect to this logic a *disruptive excess* is possible on the feminine side.

An excess that exceeds common sense only on condition that the feminine not renounce its "style." Which, of course, is not a style at all, according to the traditional way of looking at things.

This "style," or "writing," of women tends to put the torch to fetish words, proper terms, well-constructed forms. This "style" does not privilege sight; instead, it takes each figure back to its source, which is among other things *tactile*. It comes back in touch with itself in that origin without ever constituting in it, constituting itself in it, as some sort of unity. *Simultaneity* is its "proper" aspect—a proper(ty) that is never fixed in the possible identity-to-self of some form or other. It is always *fluid,* without neglecting the characteristics of fluids that are difficult to idealize: those rubbings between two infinitely near neighbors that create a dynamics. Its "style" resists and explodes every firmly established form, figure, idea or concept. Which does not mean that it lacks style, as we might be led to believe by a discursivity that cannot conceive of it. But its "style" cannot be upheld as a thesis, cannot be the object of a position.

And even the motifs of "self-touching," of "proximity," isolated as such or reduced to utterances, could effectively pass for an attempt to appropriate the feminine to discourse. We would still have to ascertain whether "touching oneself," that (self) touching, the desire for the proximate rather than for (the) proper(ty), and so on, might not imply a mode of exchange irreducible to any *centering,* any *centrism,* given the way the "self-touching" of female "self-affection" comes into play as a rebounding from one to the other without any possibility of interruption, and given that, in this interplay, proximity confounds any adequation, any appropriation.

But of course if these were only "motifs" without any work on and/or with language, the discursive economy could remain intact. How, then, are we to try to redefine this language work that would leave space for the feminine? Let us say that every dichotomizing—and at the same time redoubling—break, including the one between enunciation and utterance, has to be disrupted. Nothing is ever to be *posited* that is not also reversed and caught up again in the *supplementarity of this reversal.* To put it another way: there would no longer be either a right side or a wrong side of discourse, or even of texts, but each passing from one to the other would make audible and comprehensible even what resists the recto-verso structure that shores up common sense. If this is to be practiced for every meaning posited—for every word, utterance, sentence, but also of course for every phoneme, every letter—we need to proceed in such a way that linear reading is no longer possible: that is, the retroactive impact of the end of each word, utterance, or sentence upon its beginning must be taken into consideration in order to undo the power of its teleological effect, including its deferred action. That would hold good also for the opposition between structures of horizontality and verticality that are at work in language.

What allows us to proceed in this way is that we interpret, at each "moment," the *specular make-up* of discourse, that is, the self-reflecting (stratifiable) organization of the subject in that discourse. An organization that maintains, among other things, the break between what is perceptible and what is intelligible, and thus maintains the submission, subordination, and exploitation of the "feminine."

This language work would thus attempt to thwart any manipulation of discourse that would also leave discourse intact. Not, necessarily, in the utterance, but in its *autological presuppositions.* Its function would thus be to *cast phallocentrism, phallocratism,* loose from its moorings in order to return the masculine to its own language, leaving open the possibility of a different language. Which means that the masculine would no longer be "everything." That it could no longer, all by itself, define, circumvene, circumscribe, the properties of any thing and everything. That the right to define every value—including the abusive privilege of appropriation—would no longer belong to it.

Isn't there a political issue implicit in this interpretation of the philosophic order and this language work?

Every operation on and in philosophical language, by virtue of the very nature of that discourse—which is essentially political—possesses implications that, no matter how mediate they may be, are nonetheless politically determined.

The first question to ask is therefore the following: how can women analyze their own exploitation, inscribe their own demands, within an order prescribed by the masculine? *Is a women's politics possible within that order?* What transformation in the political process itself does it require?

In these terms, when women's movements challenge the forms and nature of political life, the contemporary play of powers and power relations, they are in fact working toward a modification of women's status. On the other hand, when these same movements aim simply for a change in the distribution of power, leaving intact the power structure itself, then they are resubjecting themselves, deliberately or not, to a phallocratic order. This latter gesture must of course be denounced, and with determination, since it may constitute a more subtly concealed exploitation of women. Indeed, that gesture plays on a certain naiveté that suggests one need only be a woman in order to remain outside phallic power.

But these questions are complex, all the more so in that women are obviously not to be expected to renounce equality in the sphere of civil rights. How can the double demand—for both equality and difference—be articulated?

Certainly not by acceptance of a choice between "class struggle" and "sexual warfare," an alternative that aims once again to minimize the question of the exploitation of women through a definition of power of the masculine type. More precisely, it implies putting off to an indefinite later date a women's "politics," a politics that would be modeled rather too simplistically on men's struggles.

It seems, in this connection, that the *relation between the system of economic oppression among social classes and the system that can be labeled patriarchal* has been subjected to very little dialectical analysis, and has been once again reduced to a hierarchical structure.

A case in point: "the first class opposition that appears in history coincides with the development of the antagonism between man and woman in monogamous marriage and the first class oppression coincides with that of the female sex by the male."[2] Or again: "With the division of labour, in which all these contradictions are implicit, and which in its turn is based on the natural division of labour in the family and on the separation of society into individual families opposed to one another, is given simultaneously the distribution, and indeed the unequal (both quantitative and qualitative) distribution, of labour and its products, hence property: the nucleus, the first form of which lies in the family, where wife and children are the slaves of the husband. This latent slavery in the family, though still very crude, is the first property, but even at this early stage it corresponds perfectly to the definition of modern economists who call it the power of disposing of the labour-power of others."[3] Of this first antagonism, this first oppression, this first form, this first property, this nucleus . . . , we may indeed say that they never signify anything but a "first moment" of history, even an elaboration—why not a mythical one?—of "origins." The fact remains that this earliest oppression is in effect even

[2]Frederick Engels, *The Origin of the Family, Private Property and the State*, trans. Alec West, rev. and ed. E. B. Leacock (New York, 1972), p. 129.

[3]Karl Marx and Friedrich Engels, *The German Ideology*, parts 1 and 3, ed. R. Pascal (New York, 1939), pp. 21–22. (*Marxist Library*, Works of Marxism-Leninism, vol. 6.) Further references to this work are identified parenthetically by page number.

today, and the problem lies in determining how it is articulated with the other oppression, if it is necessary in the long run to dichotomize them in that way, to oppose them, to subordinate one to the other, according to processes that are still strangely inseparable from an idealist logic.

For the patriarchal order is indeed the one that functions as the *organization and monopolization of private property to the benefit of the head of the family*. It is his proper name, the name of the father, that determines ownership for the family, including the wife and children. And what is required of them—for the wife, monogamy; for the children, the precedence of the male line, and specifically of the eldest son who bears the name—is also required so as to ensure "the concentration of considerable wealth in the hands of a single individual—a man" and to "bequeath this wealth to the children of that man and of no other"; which, of course, does not "in any way interfere with open or concealed polygamy on the part of the man."[4] How, then, can the analysis of women's exploitation be dissociated from the analysis of modes of appropriation?

This question arises today out of a different necessity. For male-female relations are beginning to be less concealed behind the father-mother functions. Or, more precisely, man-father/mother: because the man, by virtue of his effective participation in public exchanges, has never been reduced to a simple reproductive function. The woman, for her part, owing to her seclusion in the "home," the place of private property, has long been nothing but a mother. Today, not only her entrance into the circuits of production, but also—even more so?—the widespread availability of contraception and abortion are returning her to that impossible role: being a woman. And if contraception and abortion are spoken of most often as possible

[4] *The Origin of the Family*, p. 138.

ways of controlling, or even "mastering," the birth rate, of being a mother "by choice," the fact remains that they imply the possibility of *modifying women's social status,* and thus of modifying the modes of social relations between men and women.

But to what reality would woman correspond, independently of her reproductive function? It seems that two possible roles are available to her, roles that are occasionally or frequently contradictory. Woman could be *man's equal.* In this case she would enjoy, in a more or less near future, the same economic, social, political rights as men. She would be a potential man. But on the exchange market—especially, or exemplarily, the market of sexual exchange—woman would also have to preserve and maintain what is called *femininity.* The value of a woman would accrue to her from her maternal role, and, in addition, from her "femininity." But in fact that "femininity" is a role, an image, a value, imposed upon women by male systems of representation. In this masquerade of femininity, the woman loses herself, and loses herself by playing on her femininity. The fact remains that this masquerade requires an *effort* on her part for which she is not compensated. Unless her pleasure comes simply from being chosen as an object of consumption or of desire by masculine "subjects." And, moreover, how can she do otherwise without being "out of circulation"?

In our social order, women are "products" used and exchanged by men. Their status is that of merchandise, "commodities." How can such objects of use and transaction claim the right to speak and to participate in exchange in general? Commodities, as we all know, do not take themselves to market on their own; and if they could talk . . . So women have to remain an "infrastructure" unrecognized as such by our society and our culture. The use, consumption, and circulation of their sexualized bodies underwrite the organization and the reproduction of the social order, in which they have never taken part as "subjects."

Women are thus in a situation of *specific exploitation* with respect to exchange operations: sexual exchanges, but also economic, social, and cultural exchanges in general. A woman "enters into" these exchanges only as the object of a transaction, unless she agrees to renounce the specificity of her sex, whose "identity" is imposed on her according to models that remain foreign to her. Women's social inferiority is reinforced and complicated by the fact that woman does not have access to language, except through recourse to "masculine" systems of representation which disappropriate her from her relation to herself and to other women. The "feminine" is never to be identified except by and for the masculine, the reciprocal proposition not being "true."

But this situation of specific oppression is perhaps what can allow women today to elaborate a "critique of the political economy," inasmuch as they are in a position external to the laws of exchange, even though they are included in them as "commodities." A critique of the political economy that could not, this time, dispense with the critique of the discourse in which it is carried out, and in particular of the metaphysical presuppositions of that discourse. And one that would doubtless interpret in a different way *the impact of the economy of discourse on the analysis of relations of production.*

For, without the exploitation of the body-matter of women, what would become of the symbolic process that governs society? What modification would this process, this society, undergo, if women, who have been only objects of consumption or exchange, necessarily aphasic, were to become "speaking subjects" as well? Not, of course, in compliance with the masculine, or more precisely the phallocratic, "model."

That would not fail to challenge the discourse that lays down the law today, that legislates on everything, including sexual difference, to such an extent that the existence of another sex, of an other, that would be woman, still seems, in its terms, unimaginable.

5
Così Fan Tutti

> "The one who I presume has knowledge is the one I love."
>
> "Women don't know what they are saying, that's the whole difference between them and me."
>
> Jacques Lacan, *Encore, Le Séminaire XX*

Psychoanalytic discourse on female sexuality is the discourse of truth. A discourse that tells the truth about the logic of truth: namely, that *the feminine occurs only within models and laws devised by male subjects.* Which implies that there are not really two sexes, but only one. A single practice and representation of the sexual. With its history, its requirements, reverses, lacks, negative(s) . . . of which the female sex is the mainstay.

This model, a *phallic* one, shares the values promulgated by patriarchal society and culture, values inscribed in the philosophical corpus: property, production, order, form, unity, visibility . . . and erection.

Repeating this Western tradition to some extent unwittingly, and reproducing the scene in which it is represented, psychoanalysis brings the truth of this tradition to light, a *sexual* truth this time.

Thus, with regard to "the development of a normal woman," we learn, through Freud, that there is and can be only one

This text was originally published as "Così Fan Tutti," in *Vel,* no. 2 (August 1975).

single motivating factor behind it: "penis envy," that is, the desire to appropriate for oneself the genital organ that has a cultural monopoly on value. Since women don't have it, they can only covet the one men have, and, since they cannot possess it, they can only seek to find equivalents for it. Furthermore, they can find fulfillment only in motherhood, by bringing a child, a "penis substitute," into the world; and for the woman's happiness to be complete, the child must have a penis himself. The perfect achievement of the feminine destiny, according to Freud, lies in reproducing the male sex, at the expense of the woman's own. Indeed, in this view, woman never truly escapes from the Oedipus complex. She remains forever fixated on the desire for the father, remains subject to the father and to his law, for fear of losing his love, which is the only thing capable of giving her any value at all.[1]

But the truth of the truth about female sexuality is restated even more rigorously when psychoanalysis takes *discourse itself* as the object of its investigations. Here, anatomy is no longer available to serve, to however limited an extent, as proof-alibi for the real difference between the sexes. The sexes are now defined only as they are determined in and through language. Whose laws, it must not be forgotten, have been prescribed by male subjects for centuries.

This is what results: "There is no woman who is not excluded by the nature of things, which is the nature of words, and it must be said that, if there is something they complain a lot about at the moment, that is what it is—except that they don't know what they are saying, that's the whole difference between them and me."[2]

[1]For a presentation of Freud's positions on female sexuality, see "Psychoanalytic Theory: Another Look," Chapter 3 (above). For a detailed critique, see Luce Irigaray, *Speculum de l'autre femme* (Paris, 1974).

[2]This quotation and all other quoted passages in the rest of this section are translated from Jacques Lacan, *Encore, Le Séminaire XX* (Paris, 1975).

The statement is clear enough. Women are in a position of exclusion. And they may complain about it . . . But it is man's discourse, inasmuch as it sets forth the law—"that's the whole difference between them and me"?—which can know what there is to know about that exclusion. And which furthermore perpetuates it. Without much hope of escape, for women. Their exclusion is *internal* to an order from which nothing escapes: the order of (man's) discourse. To the objection that this discourse is perhaps not all there is, the response will be that it is women who are "not-all."

From this encircling projective machinery, no reality escapes unscathed. Alive. Every "body" is transformed by it. This is the only way for the "subject" to enjoy the body, after having chopped it up, dressed it, disguised it, mortified it in his fantasies. What is disturbing is that of these fantasies he makes laws, going so far as to confuse them with science—which no reality resists. The whole is already circumscribed and determined in and by his discourse.

"There is no prediscursive reality. Every reality is based upon and defined by a discourse. This is why it is important for us to notice what analytic discourse consists of, and not to overlook one thing, which is no doubt of limited significance, namely the fact that in this discourse we are talking about what the verb 'fuck' expresses perfectly. We are speaking about fucking—a verb, in French *foutre*—and we are saying that it's not working."

It's not working . . . Let us deal with this on the basis of logical imperatives. What poses problems in reality turns out to be justified by a logic that has already ordered reality as such. Nothing escapes the circularity of this law.

So how then are women, that "reality" that is somewhat resistant to discourse, to be defined?

"The sexualized being of these not-all women is not channeled through the body, but through what results from a logical requirement in speech. Indeed, the logic, the coherence inscribed in the fact that language exists and that it is external to the bodies that are agitated by it, in short the Other that is becoming incarnate, so to speak, as a sexualized being, requires this one-by-one procedure."

Female sexualization is thus the effect of a logical requirement, of the existence of a language that is transcendent with respect to bodies, which would necessitate, in order—nevertheless—to become incarnate, "so to speak," taking women one by one. Take that to mean that woman does not exist, but that language exists. That woman does not exist owing to the fact that language—a language—rules as master, and that she threatens—as a sort of "prediscursive reality"?—to disrupt its order.

Moreover, it is inasmuch as she does not exist that she sustains the desire of these "speaking beings" that are called men: "A man seeks a woman—this is going to strike you as odd—owing to something that is located only in discourse, since, if what I am suggesting is true, namely that woman is not-all, there is always something in her which escapes discourse."

Man seeks her out, since he has inscribed her in discourse, but as lack, as fault or flaw.

Might psychoanalysis, in its greatest logical rigor, be a negative theology? Or rather the negative of theology? Since what is postulated as the cause of desire is lack as such.

Concerning the movement of negative theology, psychoanalytic discourse also neglects the work on projections, whereby God is disinvested of worldly predicates, and of all predication. The phallic obstacle struggles against letting itself be disappropriated, and the Other will remain the place where its formations are inscribed.

But to get rid of the body, for a psychoanalyst, is not always an easy thing to do. How can the logical machinery take care of that?

Fortunately, there are women. Indeed, if the sexualized being of these "not-all" women is not a function of the body (at least not their own bodies), they will nevertheless have to serve as the object *a,* that bodily remainder. The being that is sexualized female in and through discourse is also a place for the deposit of the remainders produced by the operation of language. For this to be the case, woman has to remain a body without organs.

This being so, nothing that has to do with women's erogenous zones is of the slightest interest to the psychoanalyst. "Then they call it whatever they like, that *vaginal* pleasure, they talk about the rear pole of the opening of the uterus and other bullshit, that's the word for it."

The geography of feminine pleasure is not worth listening to. Women are not worth listening to, especially when they try to speak of their pleasure: "they don't know what they are saying," "about this pleasure, woman knows nothing," "what makes my suggestions somewhat plausible is that since we have been begging them, begging them on our knees—I was speaking last time of women analysts—to try to tell us, well, mum's the word. We've never managed to get anything out of them," "*on the subject of female sexuality, our lady analyst colleagues tell us . . . not everything*. It's quite remarkable. They haven't made the slightest progress on the question of female sexuality. There must be an internal reason for this, connected with the structure of the pleasure mechanism."

The question whether, in his logic, they can articulate anything at all, whether they can be heard, is not even raised. For raising it would mean granting that there may be some other logic, and one that upsets his own. That is, a logic that challenges mastery.

And to make sure this does not come up, the right to experience pleasure is awarded to a statue. "Just go look at Bernini's statue in Rome, you'll see right away that St. Theresa is coming, there's no doubt about it."

In Rome? So far away? To look? At a statue? Of a saint? Sculpted by a man? What pleasure are we talking about? Whose pleasure? For where the pleasure of the Theresa in question is concerned, her own writings are perhaps more telling.

But how can one "read" them when one is a "man"? The production of ejaculations of all sorts, often prematurely emitted, makes him miss, in the desire for identification with the lady, what her own pleasure might be all about.

And . . . his?

But the fact that the sexual relation is in that respect incapable of articulation is what allows him to keep on talking: "the practice of speech makes no allowance for the relation between the sexes, even though it is only from that starting point that what fills in for that relation can be articulated."

So if the relation were to come about, everything that has been stated up to now would count as an effect-symptom of its avoidance? It's all very well to know this; to hear oneself say it is not the same thing. Hence the necessary silence concerning the pleasure of those statue-women, the only ones who are acceptable in the logic of his desire.

"What does that mean?—except that a field that is nevertheless not nothing turns out to be unknown. The field in question is that of all beings who assume the status of woman—if indeed that being assumes anything at all of her own fate."

How could that "being" do so, since it is assigned within a discourse that excludes, and by its very "essence," the possibility that it might speak for itself?

So it would be a question of legislating on the relation of that being to the "body," and on the way it can be sexually enjoyed by subjects. A delicate economic problem, for it harbors non-sense. "In other words, what we're saying is that love is impossible, and that the sexual relation is engulfed in non-sense, which doesn't diminish in the slightest the interest we must take in the Other."

It is appropriate then to proceed prudently—to bed. "We're simply reduced to a little embrace, like this, we'll settle for a forearm or anything else at all—ow."

Even for so little? Pain? Surprise? Being torn apart? No doubt that part was not yet "corporealized in a signifying manner"? Not sufficiently transmuted into an "enjoying substance"?

"Do we not have here precisely what is presupposed by the psychoanalytic experience?—the substance of the body, on condition that it be defined only by what enjoys itself. A property of the living body no doubt, but we don't know what it is to be living aside from this one thing: that a body enjoys itself. It only enjoys itself by corporealizing itself in a signifying manner. Which implies something other than the *partes extra partes* of extended substance. As Sade, that sort of Kantian, emphasizes admirably, one can take pleasure only in a part of the body of the Other, for the simple reason that one has never seen a body roll itself up around the body of the Other so completely as to include and incorporate it by phagocytosis." What is at issue is thus "the *enjoying of a body,* of the body that, as Other, symbolizes it, and perhaps includes something that serves to bring about the delineation of another form of substance, the enjoying substance."

"Ow . . ." from the other side. What are we going to have to go through in order to bring about this transformation? How, how many times, are we going to have to be cut into "parts," "hammered," "recast . . ." in order to become sufficiently signifying? Substantial enough? All that without knowing anything about it. Hardly a twinge . . .

But "enjoying has this fundamental property that it is finally one body that is enjoying a part of the Other's body. But that part also enjoys—it gratifies the Other to a greater or lesser extent, but it is a fact that the Other cannot remain indifferent to it."

It is a fact. It gratifies, more or less. But that does not seem to be—for him—the question. The question lies rather in the means of attaining a more-than-corporal over-pleasure.

Over-pleasure? Surplus value? This premium of pleasure in knowledge should not—if possible . . .—make you forget the time for understanding. If you skip over this time, your ignorance gives an over-pleasure to (his) logic. Hence an under-pleasure, if only that of his knowledge. Which he enjoys—even so . . .—more than you. Allowing yourselves to be seduced too quickly, to be satisfied too soon(?), you are accomplices of the surplus value from which his speech draws an advantage over your unwilling body.

Over-pleasure has to do, during this time, with the body—of the Other. That is, for the subject, an over-pleasure of what instates it as a speaking being.

Thus her body is not at issue, "the dear woman," but rather what she is made to uphold of the operation of a language that is unaware of itself. Understand, for her, her ignorance as to what is happening to her . . .

Which he explains, moreover. "That is why I say that the imputation of the unconscious is a phenomenon of unbelievable charity. They know, they know, subjects do. But in the end, all the same, they don't know all. At the level of this not-all, there is nothing but the Other not to know. It is the Other that makes the not-all, precisely in that the Other is the element of the not-knowledgeable-at-all in this not-all. Thus, momentarily, it can be useful to hold the Other responsible for this (which is what analysis comes to in the most overt fashion, except that no one notices it): if the libido is only masculine, it is only from that place where she is whole, the dear woman—that is to say, from that place where man sees her, and only from there—that the dear woman can have an unconscious."

There it is: woman has no unconscious except the one man

gives her. Mastery clearly acknowledges itself, except that no one notices it. Enjoying a woman, psychoanalyzing a woman, amounts then, for a man, to reappropriating for himself the unconscious that he has lent her. All the same, she continues to pay, and then some . . . with her body.

An intolerable debt of which he acquits himself by fantasizing that she wants to take the part of his own body that he values most highly. In his turn he skips a logical step. If she wants something, it is by virtue of the unconscious that he has "imputed" to her. She wills nothing but what he attributes to her. If he forgets this moment when the predicate is constituted—his predicates—he is in danger of losing it as something he can enjoy. But is this not the way the renewal of his desire is assured?

"And what good does that do?" For whom? "It serves, as we all know, to get the speaking being—here reduced to man—to speak, that is—I don't know whether you have noticed this in analytic theory—to exist only as mother."

Woman as womb, the unconscious womb of man's language: for her own part, she would have no relation to "her" unconscious except one that would be marked by an essential dispossession. In absence, ecstasy, . . . and silence. Ek-sistence falling short of, or going beyond, any subject.

How, from such ravishings, does she return to the society of men? "For that pleasure in which she is not-all, that is, which makes her somewhere absent as a subject, she will find the cork in that little *a* which will be her child."

Yes, of course . . . Still . . . Without a child, no father? Nor any solution, under the law, for woman's desire? No possible (en)closing of this question in a reproductive maternal function of body-corks plugging up, solidly, the breach of the absence of sexual relations. And the abyss with which it threatens, indefinitely, any social construction, symbolic or imaginary. What—who?—are these *a* corks good for, then?

Anything, at any rate, so long as she is not a "subject," so long as she cannot disrupt through her speech, her desire, *her* pleasure, the operation of the language that lays down the law, the prevailing organization of power.

She is even granted, provided that she holds her peace, a privileged relation with "God"—meaning, with phallic circulation. So long as, by remaining absent as "subject," she lets them keep, even guarantees that they can keep, the position of mastery. However, this is a somewhat risky business . . . What if she were to discover there the cause of their cause? In the pleasure of "this *she* who does not exist and who signifies nothing"? This "she" that women might well understand, one day, as the projection onto that in-fant "being"—which they represent for him—of his relation to nihilism.

For they don't know all, the subjects. And, on the side of the cause, they might well let themselves be overrun for having made the Other bear too much of it. The problem is that they have the law, still, on their side, and they don't hesitate, when the occasion arises, to use force. . .

*

So there is, *for women*, no possible law for their pleasure. No more than there is any possible discourse. Cause, effect, goal . . . law and discourse form a single system. And if women—according to him—can say nothing, can know nothing, of their own pleasure, it is because they cannot in any way order themselves within and through a language that would be on some basis their own. Or . . . his?

Women's enjoyment is—for them, but always according to him—essentially an-archic and a-teleological. For the imperative that is imposed on them—but solely from the outside, and not without violence—is: "enjoy without law." That is to say, according to the science of psychoanalysis, without desire. When that strange state of "body" that men call women's pleasure turns up, it is gratuitous, accidental, unforeseen, "supplementary" to the essential—a state about which women know nothing, from which they do not—therefore—truly derive pleasure. But which escapes men's grasp in their phallic economy. A sort of "sensation"—a test?—that "assails" them and also "assists" them, when it happens to them.

Not entirely by chance, even so: men cannot do without that state as proof of the existence of a relation between body and soul. As symptom of the existence of a "substantive component," of a "substantive union between soul and body," whose function is ensured by the "enjoying substance."

As no intelligible entity alone can carry out this proof or test, responsibility for it has to be left to the domain of sensation. For example, to the pleasure of woman. Awoman. A body-matter marked by their signifiers, a prop for their souls-fantasies. The place where their encoding as speaking subjects is inscribed and where the "objects" of their desire are projected. The schism and the gap between those two, transferred onto her body, bring her to pleasure—in spite of everything—but do not keep her from being, or from believing herself to be, "frigid." Pleasure without pleasure: the shock of a remainder of "silent" body-matter that shakes her at intervals, in the interstices, but of which she remains ignorant. "Saying" nothing of this pleasure after all, thus not enjoying it. This is how she sustains, for them, the dual role of the impossible and the forbidden.

If there is such a thing—still—as feminine pleasure, then, it is because men need it in order to maintain themselves in their own existence. It is *useful* to them: it helps them bear what is intolerable in their world as speaking beings, to have a soul foreign to that world: a fantasmatic one. And in spite of everything, this soul is to be "patient and courageous"—a-musing qualities where fantasies are concerned. It is quite obvious who has to assume the responsibility for preserving this fantasy. Women don't have a soul: they serve as guarantee for man's.

But it does not suffice, of course, for this soul to remain simply external to their universe. It must also be rearticulated with the "body" of the speaking subject. It is *necessary* that the fusion of the soul—fantasmatic—and the body—transcribed from language—be accomplished with the help of their "instruments": in feminine sexual pleasure.

This rather spiritualistically love-laden operation has an alibi: it is accomplished by and for man only in perversion. That makes it, on the surface at least, more diabolical than contemplation of the Almighty. It remains to be seen just how that settles the question decisively. At best, does the alibi not serve to feign its deferral? A perverse decorum intervenes.

But men insist that women can say nothing of their pleasure. Thereby they confess the limit of their own knowledge. For "when one is a man, one sees in the woman partner a means of self-support, a footing on which to stand (oneself) narcissistically."

From this point on, does not that ineffable, ecstatic pleasure take the place, for men, of a Supreme Being, whom they need narcissistically but who ultimately eludes their knowledge? Does it not occupy—for them—the role of God? With the requirement, for them, that it be discreet enough not to disturb them in the logic of their desire. For God has to be there so that subjects may speak, or rather speak about him. But "He" has, for "His" part, nothing to say on this/to these subject(s). It is up to men to enact his laws. And to subject him, in particular, to their ethic.

Sexual pleasure is engulfed then in the body of the Other. It is "produced" because the Other, in part, escapes the grasp of discourse.

Phallicism compensates for this discursive crisis, sustaining itself upon the Other, nourishing itself with the Other, desiring itself through the Other, even without ever relating to it as such. A barrier, a break, a fantasmatic cutting-out, a signifying economy, an order, a law, govern the enjoyment of the body of the Other. Henceforth subject to enumeration: one by one.

Women will be taken, tested, one by one, in order to avoid non-sense. To woman's not-all in the order of the expressible in discourse there is a corresponding necessity of having them all, at least potentially, all of them, in order to make them bear the fault of the unsayable, while they dispose, even so, of that—last-born—substance called enjoying. The lack of access to discourse in the body of the Other is transformed into intervals separating all women from one another. The ek-stasy of the Other with respect to pronounceable language—which of course has to subsist as the ongoing cause of the still-corporal pleasure—is moderated, measured, mastered in the counting-up of women.

But this fault, this gap, this hole, this abyss—in the operations of discourse—will turn out to be obscured as well by another substance: extension. Subject to assessment by modern science. "The famous extended substance, complement of the (thinking) (female) Other, is not gotten rid of so easily either, since it is modern space, the stuff of pure space, like what is called pure spirit, we cannot say that this is promising."

The place of the Other, the body of the Other, will then be spelled out in topo-logy. At the point nearest to the coalescence of discourse and fantasy, in the truth of an ortho-graphy of space, the possibility of the sexual relation is going to be missed.

For to put the accent back on space was—perhaps—to restore some chance for the sexual pleasure of the other—woman. But to seek once again to make a science of it amounts to bringing it back inside the logic of the subject. To giving an over-and-beyond back over to the same. To reducing the other to the Other of the Same. Which could also be interpreted as submitting the real to the imaginary of the speaking subject.

But isn't the surest pleasure of all the pleasure of talking about love? What is more, in order to tell the truth?

"Talk about love, psychoanalytic discourse really does nothing else. And how can we help feeling that with respect to all that can be articulated since the discovery of scientific discourse, it is purely and simply a waste of time? The claim of analytic discourse—and this is perhaps, after all, the reason for its emergence at a certain point in scientific discourse—is that talking about love is in itself a pleasure."

The pleasure with which psychoanalysts are satisfied? They who know—at least those who are capable of knowing something—that there is no such thing as a sexual relation, that what has stood in its stead for centuries—consider the whole history of philosophy—is love. As this latter is an effect of language, those who know can limit themselves to dealing directly with the cause. A cause thus keeps talking . . .

And that homosexual a-musement is not about to give out. Since "there is no such thing," since "it is impossible to posit the sexual relation. Here is where the vanguard of psychoanalytic discourse is positioned, and it is on this basis that it determines the status of all the other discourses."

That the sexual relation has no *as such,* that it cannot even be *posited* as such: one cannot but subscribe to such affirmations. They amount to saying that the discourse of truth, the discourse of "de-monstration," cannot incorporate the sexual relation within the economy of its logic. But still, does that not amount to saying that there is no possible sexual relation, claiming that there is no exit from this *logos,* which is wholly assimilated to the discourse of knowledge?

Is it not, therefore, the same thing as judging the historical privilege of the *demonstrable,* the *thematizable,* the *formalizable,* to be a-historical? Might psychoanalysis remain entangled in the discourse of truth? Speaking of love, as has always been done. A little more scientifically? With a little more provision for enjoyment? And so bound once again to the speech act alone? The surest way of perpetuating the phallic economy. Which, of course, goes hand in hand with the economy of truth.

For women, that would pose a problem. They who know so little. Especially where their sex is concerned. Their sex that tells—them—nothing. It is only through the pleasure of the "body"—of the Other?—that they might articulate something. But men would understand nothing about it, because what they enjoy is the enjoyment of the organ: the phallic obstacle.

For women, the enjoyment of the "body"; for men, that of the "organ." The relation between the sexes would take place within the Same. But a bar or slash—or two?—would split them in two—or three: which would no longer be reassembled except in the workings of discourse. The truth of consciousness, the truth of the "subject" of the unconscious, the truth of the silence of the body of the Other.

Sexual intercourse between what may or may not be said of the unconscious—distinction of the sexes in terms of the way they inhabit or are inhabited by language—might be best accomplished in the analytic session. It would fail everywhere else. Because of that division of the sexes in the (sexual) relation: at the bar.

A bar which, of course, preserves the pretense that the other exists. That the other is irreducible to the same. Since the subject cannot enjoy it as such. Since the other is always lacking to itself. Can there be a better guarantee of the existence of the other? Of the Other of the Same.

For if we define the sexes in this way, are we not brought back to the traditional division between the intelligible and the perceptible? The fact that the perceptible may turn out in the end to be written with a capital letter marks its subordination to the intelligible order. To the intelligible, moreover, as the place of inscription of forms. A fact which must never be known simply.

The Other would be subject to inscription without its knowledge. As is already the case in Plato? The "receptacle" receives the marks of everything, understands and includes everything—except itself—but its relation to the intelligible is never actually established. The receptacle can reproduce everything, "mime" everything, except itself: it is the womb of mimicry. The receptacle would thus in some way know everything—since it receives everything—without knowing anything about it, and especially without knowing itself. And it would not have access to its own function with regard to language or to the signifier in general, since it would have to be the (still perceptible) support of that function. Which would give it an odd relation to ek-sistence. Ek-sisting with respect to every form (of) "subject," it would not exist in itself.

The relation to the Other of/by/in/through . . . the Other is impossible: "The Other has no Other." Which may be understood as meaning: there is no meta-language, except inasmuch as the Other *already stands for it,* suspending in its own ek-sistence the possibility of an other. For if there were some other—without that leap, necessarily ek-static, of the capital letter—the entire autoerotic, auto-positional, auto-reflexive economy . . . of the subject, or the "subject," would find itself disturbed, driven to distraction. The impossible "self-affection" of the Other by itself—of the other by herself?— would be the condition making it possible for any subject to form his/her/its desires. The Other serves as matrix/womb for the subject's signifiers; such would be the cause of its desire; of the value, also, of the instruments it uses to restore its grip on what thus defines it. But the pleasure of the organ as such would finally cut it off from the object that it seeks. The organ itself, formal and active, takes itself as its end, and thus bungles its copulation with "perceptible matter." The prerogative of technical power makes the phallus the obstacle to the sexual relation.

Besides, the only relation desired would be to the mother: to the conceiving-nourishing "body" of signifiers. Anatomy, at least, no longer encumbers the distribution of sexual roles . . . With one exception: since there is no possible woman for man's desire, since woman is defined only through the fact that he makes her uphold discourse, and especially its gap, "for that pleasure in which she is not-all, that is, which makes her somewhere absent from herself, absent as subject, she will find the cork in that little *a* that will be her child."

This quotation indeed bears repetition: anatomy is reintroduced here in the form of the necessary production of the child. A less scientistic but more strictly metaphysical postulate than in Freudian theory.

As for woman's nonexistence, "if any discourse proves it to you, it is surely analytic discourse, by putting into play this notion, that woman will be taken only *quoad matrem*. Woman comes into play in the sexual relation only as mother."

That woman is "taken only *quoad matrem*" is inscribed in the entire philosophic tradition. It is even one of the conditions of its possibility. One of the necessities, also, of its foundation: it is from (re)productive earth-mother-nature that the production of the logos will attempt to take away its power, by pointing to the power of the beginning(s) in the monopoly of the origin.

Psychoanalytic theory thus utters the truth about the status of female sexuality, and about the sexual relation. But it stops there. Refusing to interpret the historical determinants of its discourse—". . . that thing I detest for the best of reasons, that is, History"—and in particular what is implied by the up to now exclusively masculine sexualization of the application of its laws, it remains caught up in phallocentrism, which it claims to make into a universal and eternal value.

*

What remains, then, would be the pleasure of speaking of love. A pleasure already, and still, enjoyed by the ancient soul. A pleasure the science of which psychoanalytic theory would elaborate. For an over-pleasure? But of what? Of whom? And between whom and whom?

An impertinent question: pleasure could never be found in a relation. Except in a relation to the same. The narcissistic pleasure that the master, believing himself to be unique, confuses with that of the One.

How, then, can there be love, or pleasure of the other? Except by speaking to oneself about it? Circumscribing the abyss of negative theology in order to become ritualized in a style—of courtly love? Brushing against the Other as limit, but reappropriating him/her to oneself in the figures, the carvings, the signifiers, the letters of letters of love. Surrounding, adorning, engulfing, interpellating oneself with the Other, in order to speak oneself: the language of love. Speaking to oneself about it with the Other in discourse, in order to speak love to oneself.

But it must be recalled that, according to him, "courtly love appears at the point where homosexual a-musement had fallen into supreme decadence, into that sort of impossible bad dream called feudalism. At that level of political degeneration, it must have become apparent that, on the woman's side, there was something that couldn't work any more at all."

The fief, now, is discourse. "The impossible bad dream called feudalism" has not stopped trying to impose its order.

Rather it is increasingly subtle in its objects and modes of appropriation. In its ways of (re)defining domains. Of circumventing those who already have territories, lords and vassals.

From this point of view, psychoanalytic discourse, inasmuch as "it determines the real status of all other discourse," would have a chance of winning out and establishing its empire. Going back under the fences, reworking the fields, reevaluating their codes, with respect to another order—that of the unconscious—it could extend its domination over or under all the others.

So much power causes him to forget sometimes that this power comes to him only at the price of renouncing a certain model of mastery and servitude. But this discourse, like all the others—more than all the others?—that he reproduces in applying their logic to the sexual relation, perpetuates the subjection of woman. Woman for whom there would be no more space except at the very heart of discursive operations, like an unconscious subjected to the inexorable silence of an immutable reality.

There is no longer any need, then, for her to be there to court him. The ritual of courtly love can be played out in language alone. One style is enough. One that pays its respects and attention to the gaps in speech, to the not-all in discourse, to the hollowness of the Other, to the half-said, even to the truth. Not without coquetry, seductions, intrigues, enigmas, and even . . . ejaculations—whose prematurity is more or less retarded by their passage into language—punctuating the movements of identification with the lady's pleasure. "A perfectly refined way to make up for the absence of the sexual relation by pretending that we are the ones who are placing obstacles in its way."

"Courtly love is for the man, whose lady was entirely, in the most servile sense, the subject, the only way to cope elegantly with the absence of the sexual relation."

Since this relation is still impossible, according to the psychoanalyst, it is essential that ever more "elegant" procedures be fashioned to substitute for it. The problem is that they claim to make a law of this impotence itself, and continue to subject women to it.

6

The "Mechanics" of Fluids

It is already getting around—at what rate? in what contexts? in spite of what resistances?—that women diffuse themselves according to modalities scarcely compatible with the framework of the ruling symbolics. Which doesn't happen without causing some turbulence, we might even say some whirlwinds, that ought to be reconfined within solid walls of principle, to keep them from spreading to infinity. Otherwise they might even go so far as to disturb that third agency designated as the real—a transgression and confusion of boundaries that it is important to restore to their proper order.

*

So we shall have to turn back to "science" in order to ask it some questions.[1] Ask, for example, about its *historical lag in elaborating a "theory" of fluids,* and about the ensuing aporia even in mathematical formalization. A postponed reckoning that was eventually to be imputed to the real.[2]

Now if we examine the properties of fluids, we note that this "real" may well include, and in large measure, *a physical reality* that continues to resist adequate symbolization and/or that sig-

This text was originally published as "La 'mécanique' des fluides," in l'*Arc,* no. 58 (1974).

[1]The reader is advised to consult some texts on solid and fluid mechanics.

[2]Cf. the signification of the "real" in the writings of Jacques Lacan (*Ecrits, Séminaires*).

nifies the powerlessness of logic to incorporate in its writing all the characteristic features of nature. And it has often been found necessary to minimize certain of these features of nature, to envisage them, and it, only in light of an ideal status, so as to keep it/them from jamming the works of the theoretical machine.

But what division is being perpetuated here between a language that is always subject to the postulates of ideality and an empirics that has forfeited all symbolization? And how can we fail to recognize that with respect to this caesura, to the schism that underwrites the purity of logic, language remains necessarily meta-"something"? Not simply in its articulation, in its utterance, here and now, by a subject, but because, owing to his own structure and unbeknownst to him, that "subject" is already repeating normative "judgments" on a nature that is resistant to such a transcription.

And how are we to prevent the very unconscious (of the) "subject" from being prorogated as such, indeed diminished in its interpretation, by a systematics that re-marks a historical "inattention" to fluids? In other words: what structuration of (the) language does not maintain a *complicity of long standing between rationality and a mechanics of solids alone?*

Certainly the emphasis has increasingly shifted from the definition of terms to the analysis of relations among terms (Frege's theory[3] is one example among many). This has even led to the

[3]We need to ask several things about this theory: how it gets from zero to one; what role is played by the negation of negation, by the negation of contradiction, by the double reduction carried out by the successor; what is the origin of the decree that the object does not exist; what is the source of the principle of equivalence which holds that what is non-identical with itself is defined as a contradictory concept; why the question of the relation of a zero class to an empty set is evaded; and, of course, by virtue of what economy of signification is *Einheit* privileged; what does a purely objective representation leave as a residue to the subject of that representation.

recognition of *a semantics of incomplete beings:* functional symbols.

But, beyond the fact that the indeterminacy thus allowed in the proposition is subject to a general implication of the *formal* type—the variable is such only within the limits of the identity of (the) form(s) of syntax—a preponderant role is left to the *symbol of universality*—to the universal quantifier—whose modalities of recourse to the geometric still have to be examined.

Thus the "all"—of x, but also of the system—has already prescribed the "not-all" of each particular relation established, and that "all" is such only by a definition of extension that cannot get along without projection onto a given space-map, whose between(s) will be given their value(s) on the basis of punctual frames of reference.

The "place" thus turns out to have been in some way planned and punctuated for the purpose of calculating each "all," but also the "all" of the system. Unless it is allowed to extend to infinity, which rules out in advance any determination of value for either the variables or their relations.

But where does that place—of discourse—find its "greater-than-all" in order to be able to form(alize) itself in this way? To systematize itself? And won't that greater than "all" come back from its denegation—from its forclusion?—in modes that are still theo-logical? Whose relation to the feminine "not-all" remains to be articulated: *God or feminine pleasure.*

While she waits for these divine rediscoveries, awoman serves (only) as a *projective map* for the purpose of guaranteeing the totality of the system—the excess factor of its "greater than all"; she serves as *a geometric prop* for evaluating the "all" of the extension of each of its "concepts" including those that are still undetermined, serves as fixed and congealed *intervals* between their definitions in "language," and as the possibility of *establishing individual relationships* among these concepts.

All this is feasible by virtue of her "fluid" character, which has deprived her of all possibility of identity with herself within such a logic. Awoman—paradoxically?—would thus serve in the proposition as the *copulative link.* But this copula turns out to have been appropriated in advance for a project of exhaustive formalization, already subjected to the constitution of the discourse of the "subject" in set(s). And the possibility that there may be several systems modulating the order of truths (of the subject) in no way contradicts the postulate of a syntactic equivalence among these various systems. All of which have excluded from their mode of symbolization *certain properties of real fluids.*

What is left uninterpreted in the economy of fluids—the resistances brought to bear upon solids, for example—is in the end given over to God. Overlooking the properties of *real* fluids—internal frictions, pressures, movements, and so on, that is, *their specific dynamics*—leads to giving the real back to God, as only the idealizable characteristics of fluids are included in their mathematicization.

Or again: considerations *of* pure mathematics have precluded the analysis of fluids except in terms of laminated planes, solenoid movements (of a current privileging the relation to an axis), spring-points, well-points, whirlwind-points, which have only an approximate relation to reality. Leaving some *remainder.* Up to *infinity:* the center of these "movements" corresponding to zero supposes in them an infinite speed, which is *physically unacceptable.* Certainly these "theoretical" fluids have enabled the technical—also mathematical—form of analysis to progress, while losing a certain relationship to *the reality of bodies in the process.*

What consequences does this have for "science" and psychoanalytic practice?

And if anyone objects that the question, put this way, relies too heavily on metaphors, it is easy to reply that the question in fact impugns the privilege granted to metaphor (a quasi solid) over metonymy (which is much more closely allied to fluids). Or—suspending the status of truth accorded to these essentially metalinguistic "categories" and "dichotomous oppositions"—to reply that in any event all language is (also) metaphorical,[4] and that, by denying this, language fails to recognize the "subject" of the unconscious and precludes inquiry into the subjection, still in force, of that subject to a symbolization that grants *precedence to solids.*

Thus if every psychic economy is organized around the phallus (or Phallus), we may ask what this primacy owes to a teleology of reabsorption of fluid in a solidified form. The lapses of the penis do not contradict this: the penis would only be the empirical representative of a model of ideal functioning; all desire would tend toward being or having this ideal. Which is not to say that the phallus has a simple status as transcendental "object," but that it dominates, as a keystone, a system of the economy of desire marked by idealism.

And, to be sure, the "subject" cannot rid itself of it in a single thrust. Certain naive statements about (religious?) conversion—also a matter of language—to materialism are the proof and symptom of this.

From there to standardizing the psychic mechanism according to laws that subject sexuality to the absolute power of form . . .

For isn't that what we are still talking about? And how, so long as this prerogative lasts, can any articulation of sexual difference be possible? *Since what is in excess with respect to form—*

[4]But there again, we would have to reconsider the status of the metaphorical. We would have to question the laws of equivalence that are operative there. And follow what becomes of "likeness" in that particular operation of "analogy" (complex of matter-form) applicable to the physical realm, and required for the analysis of the properties of real fluids. Neither vague nor rigorous in a geometrical way, it entails an adjustment of meaning which is far from being accomplished.

for example, the feminine sex—is necessarily rejected as beneath or beyond the system currently in force.

"Woman does not exist"? In the eyes of discursivity. There remain these/her remains: God and woman, "for example." Whence that entity that has been struck dumb, but that is eloquent in its silence: the *real.*

And yet that woman-thing speaks. But not "like," not "the *same,*" not "identical with itself" nor to any x, etc. Not a "subject," unless transformed by phallocratism. It speaks "fluid," even in the paralytic undersides of that economy. Symptoms of an "it can't flow any more, it can't touch itself . . ." Of which one may understand that she imputes it to the father, and to his morphology.

Yet one must know how to listen otherwise than in good form(s) to hear what it says. That it is continuous, compressible, dilatable, viscous, conductible, diffusable, . . . That it is unending, potent and impotent owing to its resistance to the countable; that it enjoys and suffers from a greater sensitivity to pressures; that it changes—in volume or in force, for example—according to the degree of heat; that it is, in its physical reality, determined by friction between two infinitely neighboring entities—dynamics of the near and not of the proper, movements coming from the quasi contact between two unities hardly definable as such (in a coefficient of viscosity measured in poises, from Poiseuille, *sic*), and not energy of a finite system; that it allows itself to be easily traversed by flow by virtue of its conductivity to currents coming from other fluids or exerting pressure through the walls of a solid; that it mixes with bodies of a like state, sometimes dilutes itself in them in an almost homogeneous manner, which makes the distinction between the one and the other problematical; and furthermore that it is already diffuse "in itself," which disconcerts any attempt at static identification . . .

Woman thus cannot hear herself. And, if everything she says is in some way language, that does not make the lingual aspect of her speech what it signifies, all the same. That her speech may draw the possibility conditions of its meaning from its confinement to language is quite another matter.

We must add that *sound* is propagated in her at an astonishing rate, in proportion moreover to its more or less perfectly insensible character. Which results in one of two things: either the impact of signification never comes (from) there, or else it comes (from) there only in an inverted form. *Che vuoi,* then?

Without counting the zone of silence that lies outside the volume defined by the place from which discourse is projected. And meaning would have to be diffused at a speed identical to that of sound in order for all forms of envelopes—spaces of deafness to one or the other—to become null and void in the transmission of "messages." But the small variations in the rapidity of sound then run the risk of deforming and blurring language at every instant. And, if we ply language to laws of similarities, cutting it into pieces whose equality or difference we shall be able to evaluate, compare, reproduce . . . , the sound will already have lost certain of its properties.

Fluid—like that other, inside/outside of philosophical discourse—is, by nature, unstable. Unless it is subordinated to geometrism, or (?) idealized.

Woman never speaks the same way. What she emits is flowing, fluctuating. *Blurring*. And she is not listened to, unless proper meaning (meaning of the proper) is lost. Whence the resistances to that voice that overflows the "subject." Which the "subject" then congeals, freezes, in its categories until it paralyzes the voice in its flow.

"And there you have it, Gentlemen, that is why your daughters are dumb." Even if they chatter, proliferate pythically in works that only signify their aphasia, or the mimetic underside of your desire. And interpreting them where they exhibit only their muteness means subjecting them to a language that exiles them at an ever increasing distance from what perhaps they would have said to you, were already whispering to you. If only your ears were not so formless, so clogged with meaning(s), that they are closed to what does not in some way echo the already heard.

Outside of this volume already circumscribed by the signification articulated in (the father's) discourse nothing is: *awoman. Zone of silence.*

And the object a? How can it be defined with respect to the properties, also, of fluids? Since this "object" refers back most generally to a state that is theirs? Milk, luminous flow, acoustic waves, . . . not to mention the gasses inhaled, emitted, variously perfumed, of urine, saliva, blood, even plasma, and so on.

But these are not the "object *a*"s enumerated in the theory. The experts will so state. Response: will feces—variously disguised—have the privilege of serving as the paradigm for the object *a*? Must we then understand this modeling function—more or less hidden from view—of the object of desire as resulting from the passage, a successful one, from the fluid to the solid state? *The object of desire itself,* and for psychoanalysts, *would be the transformation of fluid to solid?* Which seals—this is well worth repeating—*the triumph of rationality*. Solid mechanics and rationality have maintained a relationship of very long standing, one against which fluids have never stopped arguing.

Along the same lines we might ask (ourselves) why sperm is never treated as an object *a*? Isn't the subjection of sperm to the imperatives of reproduction alone symptomatic of a preeminence historically allocated to the solid (product)? And if, in the dynamics of desire, the problem of castration intervenes—fantasy/reality of an amputation, of a "crumbling" of that solid that the penis represents—a reckoning with *sperm-fluid* as an obstacle to the generalization of an economy restricted to solids remains in suspension.

However, the terms that describe pleasure evoke the return of a repressed that disconcerts the structure of the signifying chain. *But pleasure—black-out of meaning—would be abandoned to woman.* Or awoman.

Awoman, yes, since the failure to recognize a specific economy of fluids—their resistance to solids, their "proper" dynamics—is perpetuated by psychoanalytic science. And since this may lead to the resurgence of the *cause of awoman,* a historical positioning where the fall-out of all speculation is projected. It remains to be seen just how far the compressibility of this *residue* will go.

It is true that *a good number of her/its properties have been taken over by desire, or the libido*—this time attributed by priority to the masculine. These latter are defined as *flow.*

But the fact of having taken back *in the same* the solid instrument and certain characteristics of fluids—leaving to the other only the still neglected residue of their real movements, the yet unexplained principles of a more subtle energy—poses crucial economic problems. In the absence of the relations of dynamogenic exchange or of reciprocal resistances between the one and the other, impossible choices impose themselves: either one or the other. *Either desire, or sex.* Which, thanks to the anchorage of the name-of-the-father, will produce a "friable" organ and a "well-formed" desire.

This compromise leaves each one half-solid. The perfect consistency of the sex organ does not belong to it but, by reconjugating that organ with the meaning instituted by language, it recovers a semi-solidity of desire. This operation could be designated as the *passage to a mechanics of near-solids.*

The psychic machinery would be safe. It would purr along smoothly. Of course, a few problems of entropy persist, some concern over resources of energy. But we have to trust science. And technology. All the more so since they offer possibilities for cathexes that turn the "libido" away from more embarrassing questions. If only that of the "subject's" boredom in repeating the same story over and over again.

Which is called, in part, the *death instinct.* But if we question—also, and why not?—this so peculiarly astonishing discovery of psychoanalysis, we are again led to notice *a double movement: an adaptation of certain characteristics of fluids to rationality, and a negligence of the obstacle that their own dynamics constitutes.*

You don't believe it? Because you need/want to believe in "objects" that are already solidly determined. That is, again, in yourself(-selves), accepting the silent work of death as a condition of remaining indefectibly "subject."

But consider this *principle of constancy* which is so dear to you: what "does it mean"? The avoidance of excessive inflow/outflow-excitement? Coming from the other? The search, at any price, for homeostasis? For self-regulation? The reduction, then, in the machine, of the effects of movements from/toward its outside? Which implies reversible transformations *in a closed circuit,* while discounting the variable of time, except in the mode of *repetition of a state of equilibrium.*

On the "outside," however, the machine has in some way borrowed energy (the origin of its motive force remains, partially, unexplained, eluded). And, in some way, it has borrowed its operating model. Thus certain properties of the "vital" have been deadened into the "constancy" required to give it form. But this operation cannot and must not be represented—it would be marked by a *zero* as sign or signifier, in the unconscious itself—or else it risks subverting the entire discursive economy. This latter is only saved by affirming that even what is living tends to destroy itself, and that it has to be preserved from this self-aggression by binding its energy in semisolid mechanisms.

Since historically the properties of fluids have been abandoned to the feminine, *how is the instinctual dualism articulated with the difference between the sexes?* How has it been possible even to "imagine" that this economy had the same explanatory value for both sexes? Except by falling back on the requirement that "the two" be interlocked in "the same."

And we shall indeed have to come (back) to the mode of specula(riza)tion that subtends the structure of the subject. To "the jubilant assumption of his specular image by the child at the *infans* stage, still sunk in his motor incapacity and nursling dependence," to that "symbolic matrix in which the *I* is precipitated in a primordial form," a "form [that] would have to be called the *ideal-I*," a "form [that] situates the agency of the ego, before its social determination, in a fictional direction, which will always remain irreducible for the individual alone. . . . The fact is that the total form of the body by which the subject anticipates in a mirage the maturation of his power is given to him only as *Gestalt,* that is to say, in an exteriority in which this form is certainly more constituent than constituted, but in which it appears to him above all in a contrasting size (*un relief de stature*) that fixes it and in a symmetry that inverts it, in contrast with the turbulent movements that the subject feels are animating him. Thus, this *Gestalt*— whose pregnancy should be regarded as bound up with the species, though its motor style remains scarcely recognizable—by these two aspects of its appearance, symbolizes the mental permanence of the *I,* at the same time as it prefigures its alienating destination."[5]

A considerable homage is owed for this recognition by a master of specular profit and "alienation." But too flat an ad-

[5]Jacques Lacan, "Le stade du miroir," in *Ecrits: A Selection,* trans. Alan Sheridan (New York, 1977), p. 2. No emphasis added. Further quotations from this article are indicated parenthetically within the text.

miration runs the risk of canceling the effectiveness of this step forward.

It behooves us, then, to look into the status of the "exteriority" of this form that is "constituent [more than constituted]" for the subject, into the way it serves as screen to another outside (a body other than this "total form"), into the death that it entails but in a "relief" that authorizes misapprehension, into the "symmetry" that it consecrates (as constituent) and that will cause the "mirage" of "the maturation of its power" for a subject to be always tributary of an "inversion," into the motor capacity that it paralyzes, into the process of projection that it puts into place—"a fictional direction, which will always remain irreducible for the individual alone"?—and into the phantoms that it leaves as remains. Look into that world of automatons, that robot-world which still invokes the name and even the mercy of God in order to get itself going, and invokes the existence of the living so as to imitate that existence more perfectly than is possible in nature.

For although nature of course does not lack energy, it is nonetheless incapable of possessing motive force "in itself," of enclosing it in a/its total form. Thus fluid is always in a relation of excess or lack vis-à-vis unity. It eludes the " 'Thou art that' " (p. 7). That is, any definite identification.

And *so far as the organism is concerned, what happens if the mirror provides nothing to see?* No sex, for example? So it is with the girl. And when he says that in the constituent effects of the mirror image, the sex of one's like(ness) does not matter ("it is a necessary condition for the maturation of the gonad of the female pigeon that it should see another member of its species, of either sex" [p. 3]) and also that "the mirror-image would seem to be the threshold of the visible world" (ibid.) isn't this a way of stressing that the feminine sex will be excluded from it? And that it is a sexualized, or unsexualized, male body that will determine the features of that *Gestalt,* matrix irreducible to/from the introduction of the subject in the social order. Whence its functioning according to laws so foreign to the feminine? Whence that "paranoic alienation, which dates from the deflection of the specular *I* into the social *I*" (p. 5), but whose inevitable appearance was already inscribed in the "mirror stage." The *like* prefiguring itself there as that *other of the same,* the mirage of which will forever persecute the subject with that perpetual tension between a personal ego and a formative agency that, although one's own, is unappropriable. The distinction being henceforth undecidable between which would be truly the one, which the other, which would be the double of whom, in this endless litigation over identity with oneself.

But these dissensions—intrasubjective and social—must already have left behind them, in a former time, *hysterical repressions.* And their paralytic signifying-effects. Does it follow that the question of the assumption, jubilating or not, of its specular image by a sexualized feminine body would be (in) vain? Desire having already fixed itself there, the neutralization re-marked by the "mirror stage" would be a confirmation of a "more archaic" rigidification (ibid.).

*

And if, by chance, you were to have the impression of not having yet understood everything, then perhaps you would do well to leave your ears half-open for what is in such close touch with itself that it confounds your discretion.

7

Questions

Since *Speculum* was written and published, many questions have been asked. And the present book is, in a way, a collection of questions. It does not deal with all of them . . . Nor does it "really" answer them. It pursues their questioning. It continues to interrogate. From various angles, it approaches what has been imposed or proposed in the form of questions. What can be said about a feminine sexuality "other" than the one prescribed in, and by, phallocratism? How can its language be recovered, or invented? How, for women, can the question of their sexual exploitation be articulated with the question of their social exploitation? What position can women take, today, with respect to politics? Should they intervene, or not, within, or against, institutions? How can they free themselves from their expropriation within patriarchal culture? What questions should they address to its discourse? To its theories? To its scientific disciplines? How can they "put" these questions so that they will not be once more "repressed," "censured"? But also how can they already speak (as) women? By going back through the dominant discourse. By interrogating men's "mastery." By speaking to women. And among women. Can this speaking (as) woman be written? How? . . .

Questions—among others—that question themselves and answer each other throughout this collection.

Why not leave some of them in their own words? In their immediate expression? In their oral language? Even at the price of leaving in some occasional awkwardness? Such is the case with the following transcription of a seminar that took place in March, 1975, in the Philosophy Department of the University of Toulouse. The (female) participants in the seminar had prepared a set of written questions for me. Only those that we had time to examine are included here. The complete transcript was reproduced at the initiative of Eliane Escoubas.

Some additional questions are appended. Or the same ones? Between speech and writing.

*

There are questions I really don't see how I could answer. At least not "simply." In other words, I have no intention of proceeding here with some reversal of the pedagogic relation, in which, possessing a truth about women, a theory of woman, I might answer your questions, might sit before you and answer for woman. Thus I shall not introduce any definitions into a challenged discourse.

There is one question, however, that I should like to examine at the outset. Moreover, it is the *first* question, and all the others lead back to it.

It is this one: "*Are* you *a woman?*"

A typical question.

A man's question? I don't think that a woman—unless she has been assimilated to masculine, and more specifically phallic, models—would ask me that question.

Because "*I*" am not "I," I *am* not, I am not *one.* As for *woman,* try and find out . . . In any case, in this form, that of the concept and of denomination, certainly not. (See also questions I and II).[1]

[1]These numbered "questions" appear at the end of this section.

In other words, in response to the person who asked the question, I can only refer it back to him and say: "It's your question."

The fact that I have been asked this question nevertheless allows me to hope—for it hints at this in asking if *I* am a woman—that I am perhaps to some degree "elsewhere."

When a man is about to speak in a seminar, does anyone ever begin by asking: "Are *you* a man?" In a way, that goes without saying. Someone may eventually and indirectly ask him, or more often wonder privately, whether he is "virile" or not. But will anyone ask him whether he is a man? I think not.

So the question "Are *you* a woman?" perhaps means that there is something "other." But this question can probably be raised only "on the man's side" and, if all discourse is masculine, it can be raised only in the form of a hint or suspicion. I shall not attempt to minimize that suspicion, since it may open onto a place other than that of the current operation of discourse.

I don't know whether the person who asked the question wants to try it again or not . . .

A[2] *I merely put the question forward, I didn't place it. A woman did the ordering, put it in the initial position . . .*

Let me reassure you right away, if I can. If I chose to linger over this question, it didn't imply any suspicion on my part. I seized upon it in order to try to begin to mark off a *difference*.

Of course, if I had answered: "My dear sir, how can you have such suspicions? It is perfectly clear that I am a woman," I

[2]The interlocutors are designated by capital letters—A, B, etc.—in the order of their participation. [Note of the Philosophy Department of Toulouse-le-Mirail.]

should have fallen back into the discourse of a certain "truth" and its power. And if I were claiming that what I am trying to articulate, in speech or writing, starts from the *certainty* that I am a woman, then I should be caught up once again within "phallocratic" discourse. I might well attempt to overturn it, but I should remain included within it.

Instead, I am going to make an effort—for one cannot simply leap outside that discourse—to situate myself at its borders and to move continuously from the inside to the outside.

What is a woman?

I believe I've already answered that there is no way I would "answer" that question. The question "what is . . . ?" is the question—the metaphysical question—to which the feminine does not allow itself to submit. (See questions I and II.)

Over and beyond the deconstruction of the Freudian theory of femininity, can one (can you) elaborate another concept of femininity: with a different *symbolics, a* different *unconscious, that would be "of woman" (that is,* entirely other *and not the inverse, the negative, the complement of that of man)? Can you sketch its* content?

Can anyone, can I, elaborate another, a different, concept of femininity? There is no question of another *concept* of femininity.

To claim that the feminine can be expressed in the form of a concept is to allow oneself to be caught up again in a system of "masculine" representations, in which women are trapped in a system of meaning which serves the auto-affection of the (masculine) subject. If it is really a matter of calling "femininity" into question, there is still no need to elaborate another "concept"—unless a woman is renouncing her sex and wants to speak like men. For the elaboration of a theory of woman, men, I think, suffice. In a woman('s) language, the concept as such would have no place. (See questions II.)

"Another symbolics . . ."? I am leaving symbolics aside for the moment, as we shall come back to it by another route . . .

"Another unconscious, that would be woman's"? It seems to me that the first question we have to ask is whether there is something in the unconscious as it is currently designated that might belong to the repressed feminine. In other words, before asking about elaborating an unconscious that would be *other* with respect to the unconscious as it is now defined, it is appropriate, perhaps, to ask whether the feminine may not be to a large extent included in that unconscious.

Or again: before seeking to give woman *another* unconscious, it would be necessary to know whether woman *has* an unconscious, and which one? Or whether the feminine does not, in part, consist of what is operating in the name of the unconscious? Whether a certain "specificity" of woman is not repressed/censured under cover of what is designated as the unconscious? Thus many of the characteristics attributed to the unconscious may evoke an economy of desire that would be, perhaps, "feminine." So we would need to work through the question of what the unconscious has borrowed from the feminine before we could arrive at the question of a feminine unconscious.

Moreover, supposing that this interpretation of the unconscious were carried out, and the prevailing definition of the unconscious called back into question, on the basis of what it masks and misjudges of woman's desire, through what modalities would the unconscious subsist? Would there still be any? For whom? Perhaps there would still be some for men? But what about for women? In other words, *would the operation of a "feminine symbolics" be of such a nature that the constitution of a place for what is repressed would be implied in it?*

Another question: if the unconscious consists, at present and in part, of the repressed/censured feminine element of history, the repressed/censured component of the logic of consciousness, is this unconscious not still, finally, a *property of discourse?* Whatever blows Freud may have struck against discursive logic, does not the unconscious still belong to the system of this logic? And does not this logic, which is beginning in a certain way to exhaust itself, find *reserves* for itself in the unconscious as in any form of "otherness": savages, children, the insane, women? What is the relation between the discovery and the definition of the unconscious and those "others" that have been (mis)recognized by philosophic discourse? It is not, for that discourse, a way of designating the other as an outside, but as an outside that it could still take as "object" or "theme" in order to tell the truth about it, even while maintaining in repression something of its difference?

"Can I sketch the content *of what that other unconscious, woman's, might be?"* No, of course not, since that presupposes disconnecting the feminine from the present-day economy of the unconscious. To do that would be to anticipate a certain historical process, and to slow down its interpretation and its evolution by prescribing, as of now, themes and contents for the feminine unconscious.

I might nevertheless point to one thing that has been singularly neglected, barely touched on, in the theory of the unconscious: *the relation of woman to the mother and the relation of women among themselves.* Even so, would that produce a sketch of the "content" of the "feminine" unconscious? No. It is only a question about the interpretation of the way the unconscious works. Why have psychoanalytic theory and practice been so impoverished up to now, and so reductive, on these particular questions? Can these questions be better interpreted within an economy and a logic of the patriarchal type? Within the Oedipal systematics that they presuppose?

Under what conditions is this elaboration possible? Conditions understood as historical: those of the history of the unconscious and/or psychoanalysis, and of "material" "political" history (perhaps the two "histories" might be designated as that of desire and that of its effectuality).

I think I have already begun to reply . . . About "and/or of psychoanalysis," perhaps I can offer some additional details. It seems to me that this elaboration is surely not possible so long as psychoanalysis remains within its own field. In other words, it cannot be merely intra-analytical. The problem is that psychoanalysis does not question, or questions far too little, its own historical determinants. Yet so long as it fails to put them in question, it can do nothing but continue to respond in the same way to the question of female sexuality.

The insufficient questioning of historical determinations is part and parcel, obviously, of political and material history. So long as psychoanalysis does not interpret its entrapment within a certain type of regime of property, within a certain type of discourse (to simplify, let us say that of metaphysics), within a certain type of religious mythology, it cannot raise the question of female sexuality. This latter cannot in fact be reduced to one among other isolated questions within the theoretical and practical field of psychoanalysis; rather, it requires the interpretation of the cultural capital and general economy underlying that field.

If, as Marx suggests, humanity assigns itself only those tasks that it can accomplish, can it be said, based on the current "interest" in women, that this elaboration is already under way in a practical *(or theoretical) fashion? And where?*

If I am not mistaken, Marx also says that History is the process by which man gives birth to himself.

If History is the process by which man gives birth to man, the process of man's self-generation—a statement which does not seem to me to be devoid of metaphysical presuppositions—is the statement that "humanity assigns itself only those tasks that it can accomplish" not still referring once again to men alone? Could it be otherwise in History, as Marx sees it?[3]

"Can it be said that this elaboration is already under way in a practical (or theoretical) fashion?" In that form and with that appeal to Marx, in a first phase, I can only reply: for men, perhaps . . . Perhaps, in a practical or theoretical way, they are in the process of accomplishing the task represented, for them, by the problem of women. The sign-symptom of this might be read in a certain political strategy—of the left or the right—and in certain "motifs," or problematics that are "respectable" today, even "fashionable," in the cultural marketplace.

Does this mean that the question is beginning to be resolved "on the women's side"? I think that is quite another problem. Because if, by this token alone, it were beginning to find its solution on the women's side, it would mean that there will never be any "other" woman. Woman's otherness would be reabsorbed and reduced by masculine discourse and practice. The current concern that men are evincing for women is thus, for women, at once a necessity and a danger, the risk of a redoubled alienation, for it is taking place in their language, their politics, their economy, in both the restricted and general senses.

[3]For further discussion of this question, see below, "Women on the Market," Chapter 8.

What is complicated is that there can be no "woman's discourse" produced by a woman, and that, furthermore, strictly speaking, political practice, at least currently, is masculine through and through. In order for women to be able to make themselves heard, a "radical" evolution in our way of conceptualizing and managing the political realm is required. This, of course, cannot be achieved in a single "stroke."

What mode of action is possible today, then, for women? Must their interventions remain marginal with respect to social structure as a whole?

B. *What do you mean by "marginal"?*

I am thinking especially about *women's liberation movements.* Something is being elaborated there that has to do with the "feminine," with what women-among-themselves might be, what a "women's society" might mean. If I speak of marginality, it is because, first of all, these movements to some extent keep themselves deliberately apart from institutions and from the play of forces in power, and so forth. "Outside" the already-existing power relations. Sometimes they even reject intervention—including intervention "from without"—against any institution whatsoever.

This "position" is explained by the difficulties women encounter when they try to make their voices heard in places already fixed within and by a society that has simultaneously used and excluded them, and that continues in particular to ignore the specificity of their "demands" even as it recuperates some of their themes, their very slogans. This position can be understood, too, through women's need to constitute a place to be among themselves, in order to learn to formulate their desires, in the absence of overly immediate pressures and oppressions.

Of course, certain things have been achieved for women, in large part owing to the liberation movements: liberalized contraception, abortion, and so on. These gains make it possible to raise again, differently, the question of what the social status of women might be—in particular through its differentiation from a simple reproductive-maternal function. But these contributions may always just as easily be turned against women. In other words, we cannot yet speak, in this connection, of a feminine politics, but only of certain conditions under which it may be possible. The first being an end to silence concerning the exploitation experienced by women: the systematic refusal to "keep quiet" practiced by the liberation movements. (See also questions II and III.)

If we have to speak of an other *symbolics, of an* other *unconscious (will we have to?), is this not an* other *dream of* (*the same*) symmetry?

This question seems to imply that it is absolutely unthinkable that there should be any "other." That if the advent of something "feminine" were to come about, that "feminine" would necessarily be constituted on the same model that masculine "subjects" have put into place historically. A model privileging symmetry as the possibility condition for mastery in the nonrecognition of the other. A phallocratic model. Yet as a matter of fact this "masculine" language is not understood with any precision. So long as men claim to say everything and define everything, how can anyone know what the language of the male sex might be? So long as the logic of discourse is modeled on sexual indifference, on the submission of one sex to the other, how can anything be known about the "masculine"? We may nevertheless observe that men are the ones who have imposed this model of mastery historically, and we may attempt to interpret its relation with their sexuality.

As for the priority of symmetry, it co-relates with that of the *flat mirror*—which may be used for the self-reflection of the masculine subject in language, for its constitution as subject of discourse. Now woman, starting with this flat mirror alone, can only come into being as the inverted other of the masculine subject (his *alter ego*), or as the place of emergence and veiling of the cause of his (phallic) desire, or again as lack, since her sex for the most part—and the only historically valorized part—is not subject to specularization. Thus in the advent of a "feminine" desire, this flat mirror cannot be privileged and symmetry cannot function as it does in the logic and discourse of a masculine subject. (See also question I, 3.)

In the interview with Liberation, *you object to the notion of* equality. *We agree. What do you think of the notion of "woman power"? If woman were to come to pass (in history and in the unconscious, the latter being, indeed, "only" hom[m]osexual), what would result: would* a feminine power *be purely and simply substituted for masculine power? Or would there be* peaceful coexistence? *Or what?*

Here let me propose a clarification: I think we must not be too quick to say that the unconscious is only hom(m)osexual. If the unconscious preserves or maintains any repressed, censured feminine element of the logic of consciousness and the logic of history (which add up to the same thing in the end, in a way), the unconscious is not univocally hom(m)osexual. The commonly reductive interpretation of the unconscious, along with the censure and repression maintained by it, is the hom(m)osexual factor.

It clearly cannot be a matter of substituting feminine power for masculine power. Because this reversal would still be caught up in the economy of the same, in the same economy—in which, of course, what I am trying to designate as "feminine" would not emerge. There would be a phallic "seizure of power." Which, moreover, seems impossible: women may "dream" of it, it may sometimes be accomplished marginally, in limited groups, but for society as a whole, such a substitution of power, such a reversal of power, is impossible.

Peaceful coexistence? I don't know just what that means. I don't think peaceful coexistence exists. It is the decoy of an economy of power and war. The question we might raise instead is this one: even though everything is in place and operating as if there could be nothing but the desire for "sameness," *why would there be no desire for "otherness"?* No desire for a difference that would not be repeatedly and eternally co-opted and trapped within an economy of "sameness." You may very well say that that is my dream, that it is just another dream. But why? Once again, the reversal or transfer of power would not signify the "advent" of the other, of a "feminine" other. But why would it be impossible for there to be any desire for difference, any desire for the other? Moreover, does not all reabsorption of otherness in the discourse of sameness signify a desire for difference, but a desire that would always—to speak a shamefully psychological language—"be frightening"? And which by that token would always keep "veiled"—in its phobia—the question of the difference between the sexes and of the sexual relation.

*

Now let me take up your second series of questions, about "speaking (as) woman."

"Must we say: an other *sex* = *an* other *writing*
an other *sex* = *an* other *meaning? Why?*

Can we simply oppose writing to meaning, or present them as alternatives?

B. *We are talking about supplementarity rather than alternatives. Writing and meaning: two things that intersect yet are not identical. Writing operates at the level of effects; if it is possible to speak (as) woman, writing is an effect of this. Meaning refers rather to the question of the unconscious, a feminine unconscious . . .*

Given this alternative, I haven't known how to respond . . .

The question lies rather in the equation (the "equals" sign) and not between the two formulations.

I don't know whether writing is situated on the side of the "effect" or the "cause" . . . That depends on the way this notion is interpreted. It seems to me that an *other* writing necessarily entails an *other* economy of meaning. On this basis, one may wonder whether all writing that does not question its own hierarchical relation to the difference between the sexes is not once more, as always, both productive of and produced within the economy of proper meaning. So long as it is "defined," "practiced," "monopolized" by a single sex, does not writing remain an instrument of production in an unchanged regimen of property?

But one might respond otherwise—not answer "truly". . .—by making a detour by way of Plato. In Plato, there are two *mimeses*. To simplify: there is *mimesis* as production, which would lie more in the realm of music, and there is the *mimesis* that would be already caught up in a process of *imitation, specularization, adequation,* and *reproduction*. It is the second form that is privileged throughout the history of philosophy and whose effects/symptoms, such as latency, suffering, paralysis of desire, are encountered in hysteria. The first form seems always to have been repressed, if only because it was constituted as an enclave within a "dominant" discourse. Yet it is doubtless in the direction of, and on the basis of, that first *mimesis* that the possibility of a woman's writing may come about. We shall come back to this in the questions on hysteria.

What is the double syntax (masculine-feminine)?

That phrase refers to the fact that rather than establishing a hierarchy between conscious and unconscious and subordinating one to the other, rather than ranking them as "above" and "below," Freud might instead have articulated them and made them work as two different syntaxes.

To respond from another angle: might we not say that it is because it has produced and continues to "hold" syntax that the masculine maintains mastery over discourse? Within this syntax, in this order of discourse, woman, even though she is hidden, most often hidden as woman and absent in the capacity of subject, manages to make "sense"—sensation?—manages to create "content." This syntax of discourse, of discursive logic—more generally, too, the syntax of social organization, "political" syntax—isn't this syntax always (how could it be otherwise? at least so long as there is no desire for the other) a means of masculine self-affection, or masculine self-production or reproduction, or self-generation or self-representation—himself as the self-same, as the only standard of sameness? And, as masculine auto-affection needs instruments—unlike woman, man needs instruments in order to touch himself: woman's hand, woman's sex and body, language—hasn't that syntax necessarily, according to an economic logic, exploited everything in order to caress itself? Whereas the "other" syntax, the one that would make feminine "self-affection" possible, is lacking, repressed, censured: the feminine is never affected except by and for the masculine. What we would want to put into play, then, is a syntax that would make woman's "self-affection" possible. A "self-affection" that would certainly not be reducible to the economy of sameness of the One, and for which the syntax and the meaning remain to be found. (See "This Sex Which Is Not One," Chapter 2, "The 'Mechanics' of Fluids," Chapter 6, and "When Our Lips Speak Together," Chapter 11.)

In this connection, one may very well say that everything

advanced in psychoanalysis—especially since the masturbation of little girls is conceived according to the model of "doing what the little boy does"—leaves completely aside whatever woman's "self-affection" might be. For woman does not affect herself, does not practice "self-affection" according to the masculine "model." What is "unheard-of"—and this might be one explanation, but not the only one, for the fact that the affirmation of woman as the other should come so late and that her relation to language should be so problematical—is that woman can already be affected without "instruments," that woman can touch herself "within herself," in advance of any recourse to instruments. From this point of view, to forbid her to masturbate is rather amusing. For how can a woman be forbidden to touch herself? Her sex, "in itself," touches itself all the time. On the other hand, no effort is spared to prevent this touching, to prevent her from touching herself: the valorization of the masculine sex alone, the reign of the phallus and its logic of meaning and its system of representations, these are just some of the ways woman's sex is cut off from itself and woman is deprived of her "self-affection."

Which explains, moreover, why women have no desire, why they do not know what they want: they are so irremediably cut off from their "self-affection" that from the outset, and in particular from the time of the Oedipus complex, they are exiled from themselves, and lacking any possible continuity/contiguity with their first desires/pleasures, they are imported into another economy, where they are completely unable to find themselves.

Or rather, they find themselves there, proverbially, *in masquerades*. Psychoanalysts say that masquerading corresponds to woman's desire. That seems wrong to me. I think the masquerade has to be understood as what women do in order to recuperate some element of desire, to participate in man's desire, but at the price of renouncing their own. In the masquerade, they submit to the dominant economy of desire in an attempt to remain "on the market" in spite of everything. But they are there as objects for sexual enjoyment, not as those who enjoy.

What do I mean by masquerade? In particular, what Freud calls "femininity." The belief, for example, that it is necessary to *become* a woman, a "normal" one at that, whereas a man is a man from the outset. He has only to effect his being-a-man, whereas a woman has to become a normal woman, that is, has to enter into the *masquerade of femininity*. In the last analysis, the female Oedipus complex is woman's entry into a system of values that is not hers, and in which she can "appear" and circulate only when enveloped in the needs/desires/fantasies of others, namely, men.

That having been said, what a feminine syntax might be is not simple nor easy to state, because in that "syntax" there would no longer be either subject or object, "oneness" would no longer be privileged, there would no longer be proper meanings, proper names, "proper" attributes . . . Instead, that "syntax" would involve nearness, proximity, but in such an extreme form that it would preclude any distinction of identities, any establishment of ownership, thus any form of appropriation.

Can you give some examples of that syntax?

I think the place where it could best be deciphered is in the gestural code of women's bodies. But, since their gestures are often paralyzed, or part of the masquerade, in effect, they are often difficult to "read." Except for what resists or subsists "beyond." In suffering, but also in women's laughter. And again: in what they "dare"—do or say—when they are among themselves.

That syntax may also be heard, if we don't plug our ears with meaning, in the language women use in psychoanalysis.

There are also more and more texts written by women in which another writing is beginning to assert itself, even if it is still often repressed by the dominant discourse. For my part, I tried to put that syntax into play in *Speculum,* but not simply, to the extent that a single gesture obliged me to go back through the realm of the masculine imaginary. Thus I could not, I cannot install myself just like that, serenely and directly, in that other syntactic functioning—and I do not see how any woman could.

What is the relation or the nonrelation between speaking (as) woman *and* speaking-among-women?

There may be a speaking-among-women that is still a speaking (as) man but that may also be the place where a speaking (as) woman may dare to express itself. It is certain that with women-among-themselves (and this is one of the stakes of liberation movements, when they are not organized along the lines of masculine power, and when they are not focused on demands for the seizure or the overthrow of "power"), in these places of women-among-themselves, something of a speaking (as) woman is heard. This accounts for the desire or the necessity of sexual nonintegration: the dominant language is so powerful that women do not dare to speak (as) woman outside the context of nonintegration.

What is the relation between speaking (as) woman and speaking of woman?

Speaking (as) woman is not speaking of woman. It is not a matter of producing a discourse of which woman would be the object, or the subject.

That said, by *speaking (as) woman,* one may attempt to provide a place for the "other" as feminine.

C. *Is it implicit in your discourse that the constitution of a woman's alterity implies the same thing for a man?*

If I understand your question correctly, yes. But is it up to me, I wonder, to speak of the "other" man? It's curious, because it's a question that I am constantly being asked. I find it quite amusing . . . I am constantly being asked what that "other" man will be. Why should I appropriate for myself what that "other" man would have to say? What I want and what I'm waiting to see is what men will do and say if their sexuality releases its hold on the empire of phallocratism. But this is not for a woman to anticipate, or foresee, or prescribe . . .

What already to some extent answers the next question, concerning *"speaking (as) woman and speaking (as) woman about men."* I think that speaking (as) woman has no more to say about men than about woman. It implies a different mode of articulation between masculine and feminine desire and language, but it does not signify speaking *about* men. Which would be once again a sort of reversal of the economy of discourse. Speaking (as) woman would, among other things, permit women to speak *to* men . . .

Speaking (as) woman and speaking (as) hysteric?

I should like to ask what it means "to speak (as) hysteric." Does the hysteric speak? Isn't hysteria a privileged place for preserving—but "in latency," "in sufferance"—that which does not speak? And, in particular (even according to Freud . . .), that which is not expressed in woman's relation to her mother, to herself, to other women? Those aspects of women's earliest desires that find themselves reduced to silence in terms of a culture that does not allow them to be expressed. A powerlessness to "say," upon which the Oedipus complex then superimposes the requirement of silence.

Hysteria: *it speaks* in the mode of a paralyzed gestural faculty, of an impossible and also a forbidden speech . . . It speaks as *symptoms* of an "it can't speak to or about itself" . . . And the drama of hysteria is that it is inserted schizotically between that gestural system, that desire paralyzed and enclosed within its body, and a language that it has learned in the family, in school, in society, which is in no way continuous with—nor, certainly, a metaphor for—the "movements" of its desire. Both mutism and mimicry are then left to hysteria. Hysteria is silent and at the same time it mimes. And—how could it be otherwise—miming/reproducing a language that is not its own, masculine language, it caricatures and deforms that language: it "lies," it "deceives," as women have always been reputed to do.

The problem of "speaking (as) woman" is precisely that of finding a possible continuity between that gestural expression or that speech of desire—which at present can only be identified in the form of symptoms and pathology—and a language, including a verbal language. There again, one may raise the question whether psychoanalysis has not superimposed on the hysterical symptom a code, a system of interpretation(s) which fails to correspond to the desire fixed in somatizations and in silence. In other words, does psychoanalysis offer any "cure" to hysterics beyond a surfeit of suggestions intended to adapt them, if only a little better, to masculine society?

*

Since I have begun to talk about hysteria, I shall reply briefly to the series of questions raised about this problem.

Is hysteria a feminine neurosis?

Isn't it—today, on a privileged basis—a "sufferance" of the feminine? In particular in its inarticulable relation to the desire for the mother? For the woman-mother? Which does not mean that it is found simply in women.

Is it a (feminine) neurosis?

Is the question whether it is a neurosis as opposed to a psychosis? Or whether hysteria is a pathological condition?

Each of these questions on hysteria requires at least a double response.

Is it a neurosis? Does it tend more toward neurosis? The answer is not a simple one. If it is imperative to go back to these categories, I would say that hysteria partakes just as much of psychosis, but that woman, lacking language, cannot elaborate the same system of psychosis as man. *Is it a pathological condition?* I think the response must be "yes and no." Culture, at least Western culture, constitutes it as pathological. And, since hysteria cannot be experienced outside of a social and cultural structure . . . But this "pathology" is ambiguous, because it signifies at the same time that *something else is being held back, kept in reserve.* In other words, there is always, in hysteria, both a reserve power and a paralyzed power. A power that is always already repressed, by virtue of the *subordination* of feminine desire to phallocratism; a power constrained to silence and mimicry, owing to the submission of the "perceptible," of "matter," to the intelligible and its discourse. Which occasions "pathological" effects. And in hysteria there is at the same time the possibility of another mode of "production," notably gestural and lingual; but this is maintained in latency. Perhaps as a cultural reserve yet to come . . . ?

Is there a "speaking (as) woman," a speaking of the other *woman, to be discovered behind Freudian interpretation, like the Minoan-Mycenean civilization behind that of the Greeks (cf.* Speculum, *p. 75)?*

Freud says so himself when he admits, for example, that where hysteria is concerned he failed to recognize the pre-Oedipal bond between daughter and mother. But he asserts that the daughter-mother relation is so dimmed by time, so censured/repressed, that it would be necessary, as it were, to go back to the time before Greek civilization to find the traces of another civilization that would make it possible to detect the status of that archaic desire between woman and mother.

One may also wonder about the following: if a speech of both sexes were to emerge, would hysteria still lie chiefly on the "feminine" side? Would speaking (as) woman still be on the side of hysteria? It is very difficult to reply . . .

Furthermore, I think men would have a lot to gain by being somewhat less repressive about hysteria. For in fact by repressing and censuring hysteria they have secured increased force, or, more precisely, increased power, but they have lost a great deal of their relation to their own bodies.

A. *"Sexual multiplicity," the discovery of a productive, innocent unconscious, in short, polymorphous perversity outside of any familial context—doesn't all that lead more surely away from the terrain of the old dream of symmetry and/or of the masculine imaginary?*

My first question is the following: is this sexual multiplicity analogous to the polymorphously perverse disposition of the child of which Freud speaks, or not? Polymorphous perversity analyzed by him according to a masculine model and bringing multiplicity back to the economy of sameness, oneness, to the same of the One.

We must not forget Freud's statement that "in the beginning, the little girl is a little boy." The masculine serves "from the beginning" as the model for what is described and prescribed of the girl's desire. Even before the Oedipus complex. And what Freud says—decrees as law—about the girl's castration complex holds good only if the girl can have none but masculine desires. Do you agree with this kind of assertion? And does polymorphous perversity, as analyzed by Freud, correspond to the desires/pleasures of a girl?

For example, in the description of polymorphous perversity,

there is very little question of the pleasure that may accrue from the relation to "fluids." The anal stage is already given over to the pleasure of the "solid." Yet it seems to me that the pleasure of the fluid subsists, in women, far beyond the so-called oral stage: the pleasure of "what's flowing" within her, outside of her, and indeed among women. This is only one among various possible examples, which would signify that such polymorphous perversity is still prescribed and "normalized" by masculine models. Polymorphous perversity, yes—so long as its economy is reexamined. Besides, society at large takes a repressive stance on the relation of women to anal pleasure. To be sure, women have taken up this repression on their own account more often than not. That phenomenon too needs to be reconsidered, not only in a discourse of, or about, desire, but in an interpretation of the whole sociocultural structure.

I'm saying that beyond a certain point I simply fail to understand the masculine-feminine oppositions. I don't understand what "masculine discourse" means.

Of course not, since there is no other.

The problem is that of a possible alterity in masculine discourse—or in relation to masculine discourse.

In this connection, I would like to raise another—and yet the same—question: do women rediscover their pleasure in this "economy" of the multiple? When I ask what may be happening on the women's side, I am certainly not seeking to wipe out multiplicity, since women's pleasure does not occur without that. But isn't a multiplicity that does not entail a rearticulation of the difference between the sexes bound to block or take away something of woman's pleasure? In other words, is the feminine capable, at present, of attaining this desire, which is *neutral* precisely from the viewpoint of sexual difference? Except by miming masculine desire once again. And doesn't the "desiring machine" still partly take the place of woman or the feminine? Isn't it a sort of metaphor for her/it, that men can use? Especially in terms of their relation to the techno-cratic?

Or again: can this "psychosis" be "women's"? If so, isn't it a psychosis that prevents them from acceding to sexual pleasure? At least to *their* pleasure? This is, to a pleasure different from an abstract—neuter?—pleasure of sexualized matter. That pleasure which perhaps constitutes a discovery for men, a supplement to enjoyment, in a fantasmatic "becoming-woman," but which has long been familiar to women. For them isn't the organless body a historical condition? And don't we run the risk once more of taking back from woman those as yet unterritorialized spaces where her desire might come into being? Since women have long been assigned to the task of preserving "body-matter" and the "organless," doesn't the "organless body" come to occupy the place of their own schism? Of the evacuation of woman's desire in woman's body? Of what remains endlessly "virginal" in woman's desire? To turn the "organless body" into a "cause" of sexual pleasure, isn't it necessary to have had a relation to language and to sex—to the organs—that women have never had?

What is the difference between the becoming-woman that you denounce and the feminine coming-to-be-woman? Is it that there is no question of reestablishing a difference? How would that difference escape hierarchy, and do we not remain, through difference, in hierarchy?

No, not necessarily, unless we remain within the "empire" of the same.

B. *Hierarchy presupposes sameness: difference must be masked by the same and suppressed by the same. Hierarchy presupposes identity.*

A. *It seems to me in any case that polymorphous perversity in Freud is situated at a pre-Oedipal stage in which sexual difference is not established.*

Isn't that a problem for you? Perhaps you see sexual difference as a correlative of "genitality"? That would explain a misunderstanding between us. Do we need to recall that the girl has a sexualized body different from the boy's well before the genital stage? This latter is obviously nothing but a model of normal, and normative, sexuality. When I say that we need to go back to the question of sexual difference, it is obviously not a call for a return to "genitality." But to state that there is no difference between the sexes before the genital stage is to bend the "feminine" to a much older and more powerful "model" . . .

What do you do with the question of family relations? You say that Freud neglects the daughter-mother relationship. In fact, what is the mother, where woman is concerned?

As far as the family goes, my response will be simple and clear: the family has always been the privileged locus of women's exploitation. So far as family relations are concerned, there is no ambiguity.

E. *Why couldn't the family be the privileged locus of man's alienation, in the same way?*

Of course, alienation always works both ways. But historically, appropriation isn't oriented in just any random direction. In the patriarchal family and society, man is the proprietor of woman and children. Not to recognize this is to deny all historical determinism. The same is true of the objection involving "the mother's power," as this power exists only "within" a system organized by men. In this "phallocratic" power, man loses something too: in particular, the pleasure of his own body. But, historically, within the family, it is the father-man who alienates the bodies, desires and work of woman and children by treating them as his own property.

Furthermore, when I speak of the *relation to the mother,* I mean that in our patriarchal culture the daughter is absolutely unable to control her relation to her mother. Nor can the woman control her relation to maternity, unless she reduces herself to that role alone. Your question seems to indicate that, for you, there is no difference between being a mother and a being a woman. That there is no articulation to be made, by the woman, between these two desires of hers. We would have to ask women what they think of this. Or how they "experience" it . . .

The disappearance of the family will not prevent women from giving birth to women. But there is no possibility whatsoever, within the current logic of sociocultural operations, for a daughter to situate herself with respect to her mother: because, strictly speaking, they make neither one nor two, neither has a name, meaning, sex of her own, neither can be "identified" with respect to the other. A problem that Freud dismisses "serenely" by saying that the daughter has to turn away from her mother, has to "hate" her, in order to enter into the Oedipus complex. Doesn't that mean that it is impossible—within our current value system—for a girl to achieve a satisfactory relation to the woman who has given her birth? The mother needn't be seen here in the context of the larger family. We are talking about the woman who gives birth to a daughter, who brings up a daughter. How can the relationship between these two women be articulated? Here "for example" is one place where the need for another "syntax," another "grammar" of culture is crucial.

In your work as an analyst, what do you do in order to practice speaking (as) woman?

When I speak here, in this context and in the position I am occupying, the difference is perhaps hard to detect . . . Except for—among other things—the number of perplexities, uncertainties, and questions that reveal the lack of some pre-established system by which my language would be ordered in advance? But there is simply no way I can give you an account of "speaking (as) woman"; it is spoken, but not in meta-language.

How can one be a woman, and an analyst, and a professor, for example? How can one engage in "speaking (as) woman" when some people do the talking and others listen? Here, for example, there is one person speaking and some others listening . . .

If I am speaking to you today, it is because I have already heard the questions you have asked me. But in fact, if only from the scenographic point of view, the mechanism operating here bothers me a lot. And it is perfectly clear that when I speak like this—in a seminar, a lecture, a colloquium . . .—I am obliged, compelled, to go back to the most commonly spoken form of discourse. I am trying to circumvent this discourse, trying to show that it may have an irreducible exterior. But in order to do so, it is true that I have to begin by using standard language, the dominant language.

That having been said, the form of your question is interesting in itself. It means something like this: how can one be a "woman" and be "in the street"? That is, be out in public, be public—and still more tellingly, do so in the mode of speech. We come back to the question of the family: why isn't the woman, who belongs to the private sphere, always locked up in the house? As soon as a woman leaves the house, someone starts to wonder, someone asks her: how can you be a woman and be out here at the same time? And if, as a woman who is also in public, you have the audacity to say something about *your* desire, the result is scandal and repression. You are disturbing the peace, disrupting the order of discourse. And at that point there are no two ways about it, you're shut out of the university, in fact you're excluded from all institutions (see question IV and its reply).

D. *The response of the institution is predictable, normal. But what astonishes me is your desire to be an analyst. Do you have the desire to be a woman analyst? It seems to me that it is impossible to be an analyst in the name of a desire other than that of the dominant power.*

B. *You said a little while ago that the unconscious had something to do with the feminine, and that its traditional interpretation was reductive. In order to be an analyst in the feminine mode, then, you would have to be an anti-analyst, if we take the term analyst as designating a relation to the institution and to the interpretation of the unconscious.*

Being an anti-analyst no doubt belongs to the same problematics as being an analyst in the traditional sense. Isn't the "anti-" once again, and always, understood within the economy of the same? I am not an "anti-analyst." I am trying to interpret the traditional operation of the analytic institution starting from what it fails to grasp of female sexuality, and from the masculine homosexual ideology that subtends it. And, in particular, from its relation to power.

In this sense, the traditional operation has never carried out a single analysis, to the extent that the interpretation of the unconscious reduces it to the masculine and thus obscures it, since the unconscious has something to do with the feminine. Institutional analysis is in a way not analysis at all.

That is not all I would say. I would say that, on certain points (and not minor ones), institutional analysis is reductive. It maintains itself paradoxically in sexual indifference, inasmuch as, for that analysis, the female sex is always understood on the basis of a masculine model. I would say that psychoanalysis, unfortunately, does not bring, or no longer brings, the "plague," but that it conforms too closely to a social order.

D. *Do you work within the phallocratic psychoanalytic framework—Freudian or Lacanian, it doesn't matter which—with the intention of producing a different analysis, or another mode of analytic procedure that I'll call "woman-analysis"? Or do you work in this framework so as to produce a type of listening that would not invoke the name of analysis: to destroy the analytic procedure . . .*

I could answer that the question of whether I situate myself "inside" or "outside" with respect to the institution does not concern me . . .

Do I want to produce a "woman-analysis"? Yes and no. Let us say rather that the effort is to practice listening to and interpreting the unconscious so that these pursuits no longer create hierarchical relations where sexual difference is concerned.

Among the written questions there was one asking whether I shall continue to analyze men. Of course, since it is the difference between the sexes that I am trying to bring back into play, without subordinating one to the other.

Am I seeking to destroy psychoanalysis, you asked? I am trying rather to analyze one of its modes of operation, and from that starting point to modify its practice.

G. *How, as a "woman-analyst," can you listen? I mean that up to now the analytic listening, of men or women analysts, has been situated at the level of the masculine structure of seeing, of the piercing gaze. Through what problematics, or syntax, of silence, do you position yourself so as not to "pierce"? In other words, what is the roundness of your ear, with respect to the "masculine" ear that "sees"?*

I think it is not so much, or not simply, a question of "roundness." To simplify—and, given the problems of timing, I am answering all your questions much too rapidly and allusively. . .—let me suggest that you are already answering the question . . . In what is said in analysis, one may indeed, on the traditional model of the theoretical, privilege a certain "visible" element, which goes hand in hand with truth and proper meaning . . . My ear may then be what discriminates, and identifies, and classifies, and interprets this "visible" element; it may be at the service of perception from a distance, and privilege what is "well formed." Or it may let itself be *touched differently.*

"Let itself be touched differently": does that mean touching a place that would no longer be circumscribed at the level of speech, of language in general, of the body? Is it the possibility of allowing an irradiation to be carried out on the whole of the body, on the whole of language, or making that "other" reign without naming it?

If I understand you correctly, yes. And this would mean that what is to be heard and accomplished is rather a different mode of the "syntactic," in language and in the body. Let me add that as soon as your listening ceases to privilege meaning, the well-formed, the visible, then the analyst's body, your own—in this connection we could take another look at what is called "benevolent neutrality" . . .—is no longer protected by that sort of screen or referent. And so it comes into play "differently" in transference.

It seems to me that that would be the dream of psychoanalysis.

Now here I am not sure I understand.

If the masquerade is brought back to "sameness," what is said outside the masquerade would be the "other"?

That's going a little too fast . . . but that is, I think what we are talking about. We would thus escape from a dominant *scopic* economy, we would be to a greater extent in an economy of *flow*.

If I were to write up a treatment report, as they say, I would not do it in the time-honored fashion, by "narrating," dissecting, interpreting the transference of the (male or female) analysand alone, but by restaging *both* transferences. Here is one of the things at issue in analytic power. Analysts do indeed have transferences. But either they defend themselves against them with benevolent neutrality, or in relation to the already-constituted theory, or else they ignore them completely.

Which would imply a break with the psychoanalysis of law, with the psychoanalysis of man. . .

Questions I[4]

What motivation has prompted and sustained the pursuit of your work?

I am a woman. I am a being sexualized as feminine. I am sexualized female. The motivation of my work lies in the impossibility of articulating such a statement; in the fact that its utterance is in some way senseless, inappropriate, indecent. Either because *woman* is never the attribute of the verb *to be* nor *sexualized female* a quality of *being,* or because *am a woman* is not

[4]These three questions were raised, explicitly or implicitly, by members of the jury during a doctoral thesis defense in the Philosophy Department of the University of Vincennes, on October 2, 1974.

predicated of *I,* or because *I am sexualized* excludes the feminine gender.

In other words, the articulation of the reality of my sex is impossible in discourse, and for a structural, eidetic reason. My sex is removed, at least as the property of a subject, from the predicative mechanism that assures discursive coherence.

I can thus speak intelligently as sexualized male (whether I recognize this or not) or as asexualized. Otherwise, I shall succumb to the illogicality that is proverbially attributed to women. All the statements I make are thus either borrowed from a model that leaves my sex aside—implying a continuous discrepancy between the presuppositions of my enunciation and my utterances, and signifying furthermore that, mimicking what does not correspond to my own "idea" or "model" (which moreover I don't even have), I must be quite inferior to someone who has ideas or models on his own account—or else my utterances are unintelligible according to the code in force. In that case they are likely to be labeled abnormal, even pathological.

This aporia of discourse as to the female sex—whether it is envisaged as a limit of rationality itself, or as women's powerlessness to speak coherently—raises a question and even provokes a crisis, which may be analyzed in various specific areas, but which, in order to be interpreted, have to pass through the master discourse: the one that prescribes, in the last analysis, the organization of language, the one that lays down the law to the others, including even the discourse held on the subject of these others: the discourse on discourses, philosophical discourse. In order to interrogate its stranglehold on history, its historical domination.

But this philosophical mastery—which is the issue dealt with in *Speculum*—cannot simply be approached head on, nor simply within the realm of the philosophical itself. Thus it was necessary to deploy other languages—without forgetting their own debt to philosophical language—and even to accept the condition of silence, of aphasia as a symptom—historico-hysterical, hysterico-historical—so that something of the feminine as the limit of the philosophical might finally be heard.

What method have you adopted for this research?

A delicate question. For isn't it the method, the path to knowledge, that has always also led us away, led us astray, by fraud and artifice, from woman's path, and to the point of consecrating its oblivion? This second interpretation of the term method—as detour, fraud, and artifice—is moreover its second possible translation. In order to reopen woman's path, in particular in and through language, it was therefore necessary to note the way in which the method is never as simple as it purports to be, the way in which the teleological project—the teleologically constructive project—the method takes on is always a project, conscious or not, of turning away, of deviation, and of reduction, in the artifice of sameness, of otherness. In other words, speaking at the greatest level of generality so far as philosophical methods are concerned: of the feminine.

. . . .

Thus it was necessary to destroy, but, as Rene Char wrote, with nuptial tools. The tool is not a feminine attribute. But woman may re-utilize its marks on her, in her. To put it another way: the option left to me was to *have a fling with the philosophers,* which is easier said than done . . . for what path can one take to get back inside their ever so coherent systems?

In a first phase, there is perhaps only one path, and in any case it is the one to which the female condition is assigned: that of *mimicry*. But the mimetic role itself is complex, for it presupposes that one can lend oneself to everything, if not to everyone. That one can *copy* anything at all, anyone at all, can receive all impressions, *without appropriating them to oneself,* and *without adding any*. That is, can be nothing but a possibility that the philosopher may exploit for (self-) reflection. Like the Platonic *chora,* but also the mirror of the subject.

To go back inside the philosopher's house requires, too, that one be able to fulfill the role of *matter*—mother or sister. That is, what always begins anew to nourish speculation, what functions as the *resource* of reflection—the red blood of resemblance—but also as its *waste,* as the discard that shunts what resists transparency—madness—to the outside.

Having a fling with the philosopher also entails safeguarding *those components of the mirror that cannot reflect themselves:* its backing, its brilliancy, thus its dazzlements, its ecstasies. Reproductive material and duplicating mirror, the philosopher's wife also has to underwrite that *narcissism which often extends onto a transcendental dimension*. Certainly without saying so, without knowing it. That secret in particular must never be disclosed. This role is only possible because of its ultimate avoidance of self-exploration: it entails a virginity incapable of self-reflection. And a pleasure that is wholly "divine."

The philosopher's wife must also, though in a secondary way, be beautiful, and *exhibit all the attractions of femininity,* in order to distract a gaze too often carried away by theoretical contemplations.

That woman—and, since philosophical discourse dominates history in general, *that wife/woman of every man*—is thus pledged to the service of the "philosopher's" "self" in all forms. And as far as the wedding celebration is concerned, she is in danger of being no more than the requisite mediator for the philosopher's celebrations with himself, and with his fellows.

If she can play that role so well, if it does not kill her, quite, it is because she keeps something in reserve with respect to this function. Because she still subsists, otherwise and elsewhere than there where she mimes so well what is asked of her. Because her own "self" remains foreign to the whole staging. But she doubtless needs to reenact it in order to remember what that staging has probably metabolized so thoroughly that *she* has forgotten it: her own sex. Her sex is heterogeneous to this whole economy of representation, but it is capable of interpreting that economy precisely because it has remained "outside." Because it does not postulate oneness, or sameness, or reproduction, or even representation. Because it remains somewhere else than in that general repetition where it is taken up only as *the otherness of sameness.*

By this token, woman stands indeed, as Hegel has written, for the eternal irony of the community—of men. Provided that she does not will to be their equal. That she does not enter into a discourse whose systematicity is based on her reduction into sameness.

. . . .

What are the conclusions of your work?

In conclusion, then, I come to what might be presented as propositions:

1. The fact that Freud took sexuality as the object of his discourse does not necessarily imply that he interpreted the role

of sexualization in discourse itself, his own in particular. He did not carry out an analysis of the presuppositions that bear upon the production of discourse insofar as sexual difference is concerned. Or again: the questions that Freud's practice and theory raise for the scene of representation—questions about what it represses in the form of what he designates as unconscious, questions about what it neglects as effects of overdetermination, of deferred action, "death instinct," and so on, questions about the utterances of the subject—these questions do not go so far as to include the question of the sexualized determination of that scene. Lacking such an interpretation, Freud's discourse remains caught up in a meta-physical economy.

2. From a more strictly philosophical viewpoint, one may wonder whether taking into account the sexualization of discourse does not open up the possibility of a different relation to the transcendental. Neither simply subjective nor simply objective, neither univocally centered nor decentered, neither unique nor plural, but as the place—up to now always collapsed in an ek-stasis—of what I would call the *copula*. Which requires the interpretation of being as having always already taken on (again) the role of copula in a discursive economy that denies the copulative operation between the sexes in language.

3. That place may only emerge if the feminine is granted its own "specificity" in its relation to language. Which implies a logic other than the one imposed by discursive coherence. I have attempted to practice that other "logic" in the writing of *Speculum;* I have also begun to indicate certain of its elements in "L'incontournable volume."[5] Let us say that it would reject all closure or circularity in discourse—any constitution of *archè* or of *télos;* that it would privilege the "near" rather than the "proper," but a "near" not (re)captured in the spatio-temporal

[5]In *Speculum de l'autre femme* (Paris, 1974), pp. 282–298.

economy of philosophical tradition; that it would entail a different relation to unity, to identity with self, to truth, to the same and thus to alterity, to repetition and thus to temporality; that it would retraverse "differently" the matter/form dyad, the power/act dyad, and so on. Since for the feminine, the other lies in the one [*l'un(e)*]—without any possibility of equality, identity, subordination, appropriation . . . of that one in its relation to the other. An economy of exchange in all of its modalities that has yet to be put into play.

All of this requires going back through the processes of specula(riza)tion that subtend our social and cultural organization. For relations among subjects have always had recourse, explicitly or more often implicitly, to the *flat mirror,* that is, to what privileges the relation of man to his fellow man. A flat mirror has always already subtended and traversed speculation. What effects of linear projection, of circular turning back onto the self-(as the) same, what eruptions in signifying-points of identity has it entailed? What "subject" has ever found in it, finally, its due? What "other" has been reduced by it to the hard-to-represent function of the negative? A function enveloped in that glass—and also in its void of reflections—where the historical development of discourse has been projected and reassured. Or again, a function assigned to the role of "matter," an opaque and silent matrix, a reserve for specula(riza)tions to come, a pole of a certain opposition whose fetishist dues have still not all been paid. To interpret the mirror's intervention, to discover what it may have kept suspended in an unreflected blaze of its brilliance, what it may have congealed in its decisive cut, what it may have frozen of the "other" 's flowing, and vice versa of course: this is what is at stake.

Thus it was necessary both to reexamine the domination of the specular and the speculative over history and also—since the specular is one of the irreducible dimensions of the speaking animal—to put into place a mode of specularization that allows for the relation of woman to "herself" and to her like. Which presupposes *a curved mirror,* but also one that is *folded back on itself,* with its impossible reappropriation "on the inside" of the mind, of thought, of subjectivity. Whence the *intervention of the speculum and of the concave mirror,* which disturb the staging of representation according to too-exclusively masculine parameters. For these latter exclude women from participation in exchange, except as objects or the possibility of transactions among men.

4. This brings to mind the political stake—in the restricted or generalized sense—of this work. The fact that women's "liberation" requires transforming the economic realm, and thus necessarily transforming culture and its operative agency, language. Without such an interpretation of a general grammar of culture, the feminine will never take place in history, except as a reservoir of matter and of speculation. And as Antigone has already told us, "between her and him, nothing can ever be said."

Questions II[6]

. . . *Given that you are here to "answer" about (as much as* for) *"woman"* . . .

I can answer neither *about* nor *for* "woman." If in some way I were to claim to be doing this—acceding to it, or demanding to do it—I would only have once again allowed the question of the

[6]Raised by Philippe Lacoue-Labarthe in preparation for *Dialogues,* a television program broadcast February 26, 1985. These questions are reproduced here in a very incomplete and fragmentary form. The "questions" and "answers" were exchanged in a series of letters.

feminine to comply with the discourse that keeps it repressed, censured, misunderstood at best. For it is no more a question of my making woman *the subject* or *the object* of a theory than it is of subsuming the feminine under some *generic term,* such as "woman." The feminine cannot signify itself in any proper meaning, proper name, or concept, not even that of woman. A term which I always use, moreover, in such a way as to mark its ambiguity: speaking of (a) woman underlines both the external position of the feminine with respect to the laws of discursivity, and the fact that one must all the same avoid referring it back to some empirical system that would be opaque to any language.

. . . and that I am here simply in the role of "questioner," in an exact reversal of the Socratic relation . . .

As for the "exact reversal of the Socratic relation," there can be no question of that. Even though it is important to invoke such a possibility, so as to dismiss it. The reversal—which would signify also an overturning, a reversal in relations of power—would still be played out within the same, that sameness put into place by the economy of the *logos.* In order to prevent the other—not the inversed *alter ego* of the "masculine" subject or *its* complement, or *its* supplement, but that other, woman—from being caught up again in systems of representation whose goal or teleology is to reduce her within the same, it is of course necessary to interpret *any process of reversal, of overturning,* also as an *attempt to duplicate the exclusion of what exceeds representation:* the other, woman. To put a woman in a Socratic position amounts to assigning the mastery of discourse to her. Putting her in the traditional position of the "masculine subject." More precisely, of the "subject" as phallocrat. The fact that every "theoretical" elaboration—but of course we shall have to return to the status of the theoretical—carried out by a woman is irremediably brought back to this function, the fact that it is not possible to imagine the existence of *another* such function, all of this shows clearly enough—if it still needs to be shown—that phallocracy has not ceased to center itself upon a gesture of appropriation. That anything sending messages toward or from an outside always continues to be brought back to phallocratic power and to the circularity of its discursive economy.

. . . the urgency, as I see it, of defending your work, given the type of reactions that it has provoked, and what they signify . . .

As for what is signified by the reactions that a work such as mine may provoke, I think I have just responded to that: a person who is in a position of mastery does not let go of it easily, does not even imagine any other position, which would already amount to "getting out of it." *In other words, the "masculine" is not prepared to share the initiative of discourse. It prefers to experiment with speaking, writing, enjoying* "woman" rather than leaving to that other any right to intervene, to "act," in her own interests. What remains the most completely prohibited to woman, of course, is that she should express something of her own sexual pleasure. This latter is supposed to remain *a "realm" of discourse, produced by men.* For in fact feminine pleasure signifies the greatest threat of all to masculine discourse, represents its most irreducible "exteriority," or "exterritoriality."

. . . given, as well, the position your work occupies in the contemporary theoretical field . . .

Woman has functioned most often by far as what is at stake in a transaction, usually rivalrous, between two men, her passage from father to husband included. She has functioned as merchandise, a commodity passing from one owner to another, from one consumer to another, a possible currency of exchange between one and the other. And, in recent events—my exclusion from Vincennes, for example, but not only that . . .—something of this status of the feminine has indeed thus been "played out." In what arena, then, is woman situated? Who or what is her "father"? What is her "proper name"? To whom does she belong? What "family" or "clientele" does she come from? If all this is not clearly settled, the only way to maintain the economy in place is by rejecting the feminine. Of course, commodities should never speak, and certainly should not go to market alone. For such actions turn out to be totally subversive to the economy of exchange among subjects.

. . . what is implied when a woman enters into the "theory of woman" or into the deconstruction of the "theory of woman"?

It is not correct to say that I have "entered into" the "theory of woman," or even simply into its deconstruction. For, in that particular marketplace, I have nothing to say. I am only supposed to keep commerce going by being an object of consumption or exchange. What seems difficult or even impossible to imagine is that there could be some other mode of exchange(s) that might not obey the same logic. Yet that is the condition for the emergence of something of woman's language and woman's pleasure. But it would have to happen "elsewhere," in some place other than that of women's integration and recapture within the economy of purely masculine desire. In other words, we could not speak of (a) woman "entering into" any theory whatsoever unless the theory in question were to become an "enactment" of the copula, and not an appropriation of/by being. But then we would no longer be dealing either with entrances or with theories. And all the reactions of scorn, silence, rejection, and at the same time exploitation of a woman's "work" in order to find the language of her pleasure offer sufficient proof that we are not quite there.

Why speak (dialogue) here with a man, and a man whose craft is after all philosophy?

Why try to speak with a man? Because what I want, in fact, is not to create a theory of woman, but to secure a place for the feminine within sexual difference. That difference—masculine/feminine—has always operated "within" systems that are representative, self-representative, of the (masculine) subject. Moreover, these systems have produced many other differences that appear articulated to compensate for an operative sexual indifference. For one sex and its lack, its atrophy, its negative, still does not add up to two. In other words, the feminine has never been defined except as the inverse, indeed the underside, of the masculine. So for woman it is not a matter of installing herself within this lack, this negative, even by denouncing it, nor of reversing the economy of sameness by turning the feminine into *the standard for "sexual difference";* it is rather a matter of trying to practice that difference. Hence these questions: what other mode of reading or writing, of interpretation and affirmation, may be mine inasmuch as I am a woman, with respect to you, a man? Is it possible that the difference might not be reduced once again to a process of *hierarchization? Of subordinating the other to the same?*

As for philosophy, so far as the question of woman is concerned—and it comes down to the question of sexual difference—this is indeed what has to be brought into question. Unless we are to agree naively—or perhaps strategically—to limit ourselves to some narrow sphere, some marginal area that would leave intact the discourse that lays down the law to all the others: philosophical discourse. The philosophical order is indeed the one that has to be questioned, and *disturbed,* inasmuch as it covers over sexual difference. Having failed to provide an adequate interpretation of the sway philosophical discourse holds over all the rest, psychoanalysis itself has committed its theory and practice to a misunderstanding of the difference between the sexes. Psychoanalytic practice and theory certainly pose a challenge to philosophical discursivity, but they still might be reincorporated into it to a large extent—as indeed they are—if it were not for the "question" of female sexuality. So it is both because psychoanalysis still constitutes a possible enclave of philosophical discourse, and because as a woman I cannot agree to it, that I am resisting this reappropriation, that I have wanted this "dialogue" with a male philosopher, a man who is also interested in psychoanalytic theory, in the question of woman, and, of course, in the question of appropriation.

What is the signification of this gesture with respect to everything that may be called today, on whatever basis, a "women's liberation movement"? Why this separatist breaking away of "women-among-themselves"?

The signification of this gesture with respect to women's liberation movements? Let's say that at first glance it may look like a breaking away, as you put it. This would mean that the empirical fact of remaining always and only among women would be necessary and even sufficient to put one on the side of "women's liberation," politically . . . But wouldn't it still be maintaining an idealist logic to pose the alternative in those terms: women either function alongside men, where they will be no more than objects, images, ideas, aspects of a feeling-matter appropriated by and for men, or else—but isn't this "or else" in danger of amounting finally to the same thing?—women remain among themselves. Which is not to say that they have no compelling need to do this. As a political tactic in particular. Women—as the stakes of private property, of appropriation by and for discourse—have always been put in a position of mutual rivalry. So to make their own efforts more effective, they have had to constitute a place where they could be "among themselves." A place for individual and collective "consciousness-raising" concerning the specific oppression of women, a place where the desire of women by and for each other could be recognized, a place for them to regroup. But, for me, that place is in danger of becoming a utopia of historical reversal, a dream of reappropriation of power—particularly phallic power—by women if it closes itself in on the circle of its demands and even desires. And besides, it would just be copying the society of men among themselves, with women remaining once again in the role assigned to them. Except that women could do without men while they are elaborating their own society?

So the "breaking away" of which you speak—and which, for me, is not one—seems strategically necessary, too, for two reasons at least: 1. Women cannot work on the question of their own oppression without an analysis and even an experience of institutions—institutions governed by men. 2. What poses a problem—a fundamental one?—for the feminine, hence the necessity and usefulness of this angle of approach, is the operation of discursive logic. For example, in its oppositions, its schisms, between empirical and transcendental, perceptible and intelligible, matter and idea, and so on. That hierarchical structure has always put the feminine in a position of inferiority, of exploitation, of exclusion with respect to language. But, in the same stroke, as it were, it has confirmed the impracticable character of the sexual relation. For this relation boils down to man's self-affection mediated by the feminine, which he has appropriated into his language. The reciprocal not being "true." Thus it is necessary to turn again to this "proper" character of language, analyzing it not only in its dual movement of appropriation and disappropriation with respect to the masculine subject alone, but also in what remains mute, and deprived of any possibility of "self-affection," of "self-representation," for the feminine. If the only response to men-among-themselves is women-among-themselves, whatever subtends the functioning of the logic of presence, of being, of property—and thus maintains the effacement of the difference between the sexes—is very likely to perpetuate and even reinforce itself. Rather than maintaining the masculine-feminine opposition, it would be appropriate to seek a possibility of *nonhierarchical* articulation of that difference in language. This explains what you call the breaking away of "women-among-themselves"; such a break is equally necessary where "men-among-themselves" are concerned, even though it is more difficult to bring about, since that state of affairs underlies the contemporary forms of their power.

One cannot fail to have at least a sense that your first concern is to avoid a naive positioning of "the question of women." One that would be, for example, a pure and simple reversal of the masculine positioning of the question (a pure and simple reversal of "phallogocentrism," and so forth).

To this question I think I have in fact already replied, both in answering the preceding questions and in writing *Speculum*. Which is obviously not a book *about* woman; and it is still less-whatever one may think about it, or even project from it as a hope for the reversal of values—a "studied gynecocentrism," a "place of the monopolization of the symbolic" to the benefit of a woman, or of some women. Such naive judgments overlook the fact that from a feminine locus nothing can be articulated without a questioning of the symbolic itself. But we do not escape so easily from reversal. We do not escape, in particular, by thinking we can dispense with a rigorous interpretation of phallogocentrism. There is no simple manageable way to leap to the outside of phallogocentrism, *nor any possible way to situate oneself there, that would result from the simple fact of being a woman*. And in *Speculum*, if I was attempting to move back through the "masculine" imaginary, that is, our cultural imaginary, it is because that move imposed itself, both in order to demarcate the possible "outside" of this imaginary and to allow me to situate myself with respect to it as a woman, implicated in it and at the same time exceeding its limits. But I see this excess, of course, as what makes the sexual relation possible, and not as a reversal of phallic power. And my "first" reaction to this excess is to laugh. Isn't laughter the first form of liberation from a secular oppression? *Isn't the phallic tantamount to the seriousness of meaning?* Perhaps woman, and the sexual relation, transcend it "first" in laughter?

Besides, women among themselves begin by laughing. To escape from a pure and simple reversal of the masculine position means in any case not to forget to laugh. Not to forget that the dimension of desire, of pleasure, is untranslatable, unrepresentable, irrecuperable, in the "seriousness"—the adequacy, the univocity, the truth . . .—of a discourse that claims to state its meaning. Whether it is produced by men or women. Which is not to assert that one has to give in to saying just anything at all, but that *speaking the truth constitutes the prohibition on woman's pleasure, and thus on the sexual relation.* The covering-up of its forcefulness, of force itself, under the lawmaking power of discourse. Moreover, it is right here that the most virulent issue at stake in the oppression of women is located today: men want to hold onto the initiative of discourse about sexual pleasure, and thus also about *her* pleasure.

Question III[7]

Can you say something about your work in relation to the women's liberation movement?

Before attempting to answer your question, I should like to clarify two things:

[7]A question raised by Hans Reitzels Forlag and Fredrik Engelstad during an interview published by the Pax Press in Oslo.

—First, that I can't tell you what is happening in the liberation movement. Even granting that I might wish to answer your question, what is happening in the women's liberation movement cannot simply be surveyed, described, related "from the outside."

—Second, that I prefer to speak, in the plural, of women's liberation movement*s*. In fact, there are multiple groups and tendencies in women's struggles today, and to reduce them to a single movement involves a risk of introducing phenomena of hierarchization, claims of orthodoxy, and so on.

To come back to my work: I am trying, as I have already indicated, to go back through the masculine imaginary, to interpret the way it has reduced us to silence, to muteness or mimicry, and I am attempting, from that starting-point and at the same time, to (re)discover a possible space for the feminine imaginary.

But it is obviously not simply an "individual" task. A long history has put all women in the same sexual, social, and cultural condition. Whatever inequalities may exist among women, they all undergo, even without clearly realizing it, the same oppression, the same exploitation of their body, the same denial of their desire.

That is why it is very important for women to be able to join together, and to join together "among themselves." In order to begin to escape from the spaces, roles, and gestures that they have been assigned and taught by the society of men. In order to love each other, even though men have organized a *de facto* rivalry among women. In order to discover a form of "social existence" other than the one that has always been imposed upon them. The first issue facing liberation movements is that of making each woman "conscious" of the fact that what she has felt in her personal experience is a condition shared by all women, thus *allowing that experience to be politicized.*

But what does "political" mean, here? No "women's politics" exists, not yet, at least not in the broad sense. And, if such a politics comes into existence one of these days, it will be very different from the politics instituted by men. For the questions raised by the exploitation of women's bodies exceed the stakes, the schemas, and of course the "parties" of the politics known and practiced up to now. Obviously, that does not prevent political parties from wanting to "co-opt" the woman question by granting women a place in their ranks, with the aim of aligning them—one more time . . .—with their "programs," which, most of the time, have nothing to do with them, in the sense that these programs fail to take into consideration the *specific exploitation* of women. For the exploitation of women does not constitute a *limited* question, within politics, one which would concern only a "sector" of the population, or a "part" of the "body politic." When women want to escape from exploitation, they do not merely destroy a few "prejudices," they disrupt the entire order of dominant values, economic, social, moral, and sexual. They call into question all existing theory, all thought, all language, inasmuch as these are monopolized by men and men alone. They challenge *the very foundation of our social and cultural order,* whose organization has been prescribed by the patriarchal system.

The patriarchal foundation of our social existence is in fact overlooked in contemporary politics, even leftist politics. Up to now *even Marxism has paid very little attention to the problems of the specific exploitation of women, and women's struggles most often seem to disturb the Marxists.* Even though these struggles could be interpreted with the help of the schemas for the analysis of social exploitation to which Marxist political programs lay specific claim. Provided, of course, that these schemas be used differently. But no politics has, up to now, questioned its own relation to phallocratic power . . .

In concrete terms, that means that women must of course continue to struggle for equal wages and social rights, against discrimination in employment and education, and so forth. But that is not enough: women merely "equal" to men would be "like them," therefore not women. Once more, the difference between the sexes would be in that way canceled out, ignored, papered over. So it is essential for women among themselves to invent new modes of organization, new forms of struggle, new challenges. The various liberation movements have already begun to do this, and a "women's international" is beginning to take shape. But here too, innovation is necessary: institutions, hierarchy, and authority—that is, the existing forms of politics—are men's affairs. Not ours.

That explains certain difficulties encountered by the liberation movements. If women allow themselves to be caught in the trap of power, in the game of authority, if they allow themselves to be contaminated by the "paranoid" operations of masculine politics, they have nothing more to say or do *as women.* That is why one of the tasks in France today is to try to regroup the movement's various tendencies around a certain number of specific themes and actions: rape, abortion, the challenge to the prerogative of the father's name in the case of juridical decisions that determine "to whom children belong," the full-fledged participation of women in legislative decisions and actions, and so on. And yet all that must never disguise the fact that it is in order to bring their difference to light that women are demanding their rights.

For my part, I refuse to let myself be locked into a single "group" within the women's liberation movement. Especially if such a group becomes ensnared in the exercise of power, if it purports to determine the "truth" of the feminine, to legislate as to what it means to "be a woman," and to condemn women who might have immediate objectives that differ from theirs. I think the most important thing to do is to expose the exploitation common to all women and to find the struggles that are appropriate for each woman, right where she is, depending upon her nationality, her job, her social class, her sexual experience, that is, upon the form of oppression that is for her the most immediately unbearable.

Question IV[8]

What do you propose to do in your teaching?

In order to stage what is at stake in this task, I shall once again take the figure of Antigone—in Sophocles, Hölderlin, Hegel, and Brecht—as my point of departure. I shall attempt to analyze what Antigone supports, shores up, in the operation of the law. How by confronting the discourse that lays down the law she makes manifest that subterranean supporting structure that she is preserving, that other "face" of discourse that causes a crisis when it appears in broad daylight. Whence her being sent off to death, her "burial" in oblivion, the repression—censure?—of the values that she represents for the City-State: the relation to the "divine," to the unconscious, to red blood (which has to nourish re-semblance, but without making any stain on it).

Why, then, has the verdict of the King and the City-State, of Knowledge and discursivity—but also of her brothers and her

[8]In a departure from the usual practice, this question was addressed to instructors by the "Department of Psychoanalysis" of the University of Vincennes before its "restructuring" in the fall of 1974. A commission of three members named by Jacques Lacan wrote me without further explanation that my project "could not be accepted." I who had been an instructor in the department since the founding of the University of Vincennes thus was suspended from my teaching. These clarifications would not have been necessary if a version contrary to the facts had not been circulated both in France and abroad.

sisters—always been to condemn her to death in order to assure his/its/their power? Must one see in that penalty the effects of a historical era? Or the *constituent necessities of rationality?* In what respect are these latter causing a problem at the present time, and even provoking a crisis?

What is the position of psychoanalytic discourse with respect to that problem, that crisis? Even if it does allow what is at stake to be more rigorously interpreted, *does it grant a different status to feminine desire?* Does it grant women a language other than that of the hysteric, which is a matter for speculation?

These questions will orient a rereading of psychoanalytic discourse on female sexuality, and especially on the difference between the sexes and its articulation in language.

This undertaking could also be set forth in the following terms. The discourse of psychoanalysis carries out a repetition/interpretation of the function historically allocated to woman. What has been needed, in effect, is a discourse in which sexuality itself is at stake so that what has been serving as a condition of possibility of philosophical discourse, of rationality in general, can make itself heard.

If, in addition and at the same time, one takes into consideration the *contributions of the science of language*—but also its aporias—one is led back to the problem of enunciation in the production of discourse. To the fact that this latter speaks of the unconscious, but also to the question: *what is the status of the effects of sexualization on discourse?* In other words, *is sexual difference marked in the functioning of language, and how?* It is thus a matter of examining the texts of psychoanalytic discourse in order to read what they express—and how?—of female sexuality, and even more of sexual difference.

This reading is one more interpretive rereading of philosophical discourse, based on a factoring in of the unconscious and its economy. But since philosophical discourse has set forth the laws of the order of discourse, it will be necessary to go back through its decisive moments looking at the status imparted to the feminine within discursive systematicity, *so that psychoanalytic interpretation will not fall back into the norms of philosophical discursivity*. In particular as regards the function that is assumed there by the "other": in the most general terms, the feminine. The question being how to detach the other—woman—from the otherness of sameness.

Philosophy, as the discourse on discourse, has also largely governed the discourse of science. From this viewpoint, *the historical lag in the mathematization of fluids as compared to solids* leads back to the same type of problem: why has solid mechanics prevailed over fluid mechanics, and what complicity does that order of things maintain with rationality? (See above, "The 'Mechanics' of Fluids," Chapter 6.)

What does this dominant rationality make of woman? Only "awoman"; "woman does not exist" (Jacques Lacan). A point of view which can be heard loud and clear at last in psychoanalytic discourse.

8

Women on the Market

The society we know, our own culture, is based upon the exchange of women. Without the exchange of women, we are told, we would fall back into the anarchy (?) of the natural world, the randomness (?) of the animal kingdom. The passage into the social order, into the symbolic order, into order as such, is assured by the fact that men, or groups of men, circulate women among themselves, according to a rule known as the incest taboo.

Whatever familial form this prohibition may take in a given state of society, its signification has a much broader impact. It assures the foundation of the economic, social, and cultural order that has been ours for centuries.

Why exchange women? Because they are "scarce [commodities] . . . essential to the life of the group," the anthropologist tells us.[1] Why this characteristic of scarcity, given the biological equilibrium between male and female births? Because the "deep polygamous tendency, which exists among all men, always makes the number of available women seem insufficient. Let us add that, even if there were as many women as men, these women would not all be equally desirable . . . and that, by definition . . . , the most desirable women must form a minority."[2]

This text was originally published as "Le marché des femmes," in *Sessualità e politica,* (Milan: Feltrinelli, 1978).

[1]Claude Lévi-Strauss, *The Elementary Structures of Kinship* (*Les Structures élémentaires de la Parenté,* 1949, rev. 1967), trans. James Harle Bell, John Richard von Sturmer, and Rodney Needham (Boston, 1969), p. 36.

[2]Ibid., p. 38.

Are men all equally desirable? Do women have no tendency toward polygamy? The good anthropologist does not raise such questions. *A fortiori:* why are men not objects of exchange among women? It is because women's bodies—through their use, consumption, and circulation—provide for the condition making social life and culture possible, although they remain an unknown "infrastructure" of the elaboration of that social life and culture. The exploitation of the matter that has been sexualized female is so integral a part of our sociocultural horizon that there is no way to interpret it except within this horizon.

In still other words: all the systems of exchange that organize patriarchal societies and all the modalities of productive work that are recognized, valued, and rewarded in these societies are men's business. The production of women, signs, and commodities is always referred back to men (when a man buys a girl, he "pays" the father or the brother, not the mother . . .), and they always pass from one man to another, from one group of men to another. The work force is thus always assumed to be masculine, and "products" are objects to be used, objects of transaction among men alone.

Which means that the possibility of our social life, of our culture, depends upon a ho(m)mo-sexual monopoly? The law that orders our society is the exclusive valorization of men's needs/desires, of exchanges among men. What the anthropologist calls the passage from nature to culture thus amounts to the institution of the reign of hom(m)o-sexuality. Not in an "immediate" practice, but in its "social" mediation. From this point on, patriarchal societies might be interpreted as societies functioning in the mode of "semblance." The value of symbolic and imaginary productions is superimposed upon, and even substituted for, the value of relations of material, natural, and corporal (re)production.

In this new matrix of History, in which man begets man as

his own likeness, wives, daughters, and sisters have value only in that they serve as the possibility of, and potential benefit in, relations among men. The use of and traffic in women subtend and uphold the reign of masculine hom(m)o-sexuality, even while they maintain that hom(m)o-sexuality in speculations, mirror games, identifications, and more or less rivalrous appropriations, which defer its real practice. Reigning everywhere, although prohibited in practice, hom(m)o-sexuality is played out through the bodies of women, matter, or sign, and heterosexuality has been up to now just an alibi for the smooth workings of man's relations with himself, of relations among men. Whose "sociocultural endogamy" excludes the participation of that other, so foreign to the social order: woman. Exogamy doubtless requires that one leave one's family, tribe, or clan, in order to make alliances. All the same, it does not tolerate marriage with populations that are too far away, too far removed from the prevailing cultural rules. A sociocultural endogamy would thus forbid commerce *with* women. Men make commerce *of* them, but they do not enter into any exchanges *with* them. Is this perhaps all the more true because exogamy is an economic issue, perhaps even subtends economy as such? The exchange of women as goods accompanies and stimulates exchanges of other "wealth" among groups of men. The economy—in both the narrow and the broad sense—that is in place in our societies thus requires that women lend themselves to alienation in consumption, and to exchanges in which they do not participate, and that men be exempt from being used and circulated like commodities.

*

Marx's analysis of commodities as the elementary form of capitalist wealth can thus be understood as an interpretation of the status of woman in so-called partriarchal societies. The organization of such societies, and the operation of the symbolic system on which this organization is based—a symbolic system whose instrument and representative is the proper name: the name of the father, the name of God—contain in a nuclear form the developments that Marx defines as characteristic of a capitalist regime: the submission of "nature" to a "labor" on the part of men who thus constitute "nature" as use value and exchange value; the division of labor among private producer-owners who exchange their women-commodities among themselves, but also among producers and exploiters or exploitees of the social order; the standardization of women according to proper names that determine their equivalences; a tendency to accumulate wealth, that is, a tendency for the representatives of the most "proper" names—the leaders—to capitalize more women than the others; a progression of the social work of the symbolic toward greater and greater abstraction; and so forth.

To be sure, the means of production have evolved, new techniques have been developed, but it does seem that as soon as the father-man was assured of his reproductive power and had marked his products with his name, that is, from the very origin of private property and the patriarchal family, social exploitation occurred. In other words, all the social regimes of "History" are based upon the exploitation of one "class" of producers, namely, women. Whose reproductive use value (reproductive of children and of the labor force) and whose constitution as exchange value underwrite the symbolic order as such, without any compensation in kind going to them for that "work." For such compensation would imply a double system of exchange, that is, a shattering of the monopolization of the proper name (and of what it signifies as appropriative power) by father-men.

Thus the social body would be redistributed into producer-subjects no longer functioning as commodities because they provided the standard of value for commodities, and into commodity-objects that ensured the circulation of exchange without participating in it as subjects.

*

Let us now reconsider a few points[3] in Marx's analysis of value that seem to describe the social status of women.

Wealth amounts to a subordination of the use of things to their accumulation. Then would *the way women are used matter less than their number?* The possession of a woman is certainly indispensable to man for the reproductive use value that she represents; but what he desires is to have them all. To "accumulate" them, to be able to count off his conquests, seductions, possessions, both sequentially and cumulatively, as measure or standard(s).

All but one? For if the series could be closed, value might well lie, as Marx says, in the relation among them rather than in the relation to a standard that remains external to them—whether gold or phallus.

The use made of women is thus of less value than their appropriation one by one. And their "usefulness" is not what counts the most. Woman's price is not determined by the "properties"

[3]These notes constitute a statement of points that will be developed in a subsequent chapter. All the quotations in the remainder of this chapter are excerpted from Marx's *Capital,* section 1, chapter 1. (The page numbers given in the text refer to the Modern Library edition, trans. Samuel Moore and Edward Aveling, ed. Frederick Engels, rev. Ernest Untermann [New York, 1906].) Will it be objected that this interpretation is analogical by nature? I accept the question, on condition that it be addressed also, and in the first place, to Marx's analysis of commodities. Did not Aristotle, a "great thinker" according to Marx, determine the relation of form to matter by analogy with the relation between masculine and feminine? Returning to the question of the difference between the sexes would amount instead, then, to going back through analogism.

of her body—although her body constitutes the *material* support of that price.

But when women are exchanged, woman's body must be treated as an *abstraction*. The exchange operation cannot take place in terms of some intrinsic, immanent value of the commodity. It can only come about when two objects—two women—are in a relation of equality with a third term that is neither the one nor the other. It is thus not as "women" that they are exchanged, but as women reduced to some common feature—their current price in gold, or phalluses—and of which they would represent a plus or minus quantity. Not a plus or a minus of feminine qualities, obviously. Since these qualities are abandoned in the long run to the needs of the consumer, *woman has value on the market by virtue of one single quality: that of being a product of man's "labor."*

On this basis, each one looks exactly like every other. They all have the same phantom-like reality. Metamorphosed in identical *sublimations,* samples of the same indistinguishable work, all these objects now manifest just one thing, namely, that in their production a force of human labor has been expended, that labor has accumulated in them. In their role as crystals of that common social substance, they are deemed to have value.

As commodities, women are thus two things at once: utilitarian objects and bearers of value. "They manifest themselves therefore as commodities, or have the form of commodities, only in so far as they have two forms, a physical or natural form, and a value form" (p. 55).

But "the reality of the value of commodities differs in this respect from Dame Quickly, that we don't know 'where to have it' " (ibid.). *Woman, object of exchange, differs from woman, use value, in that one doesn't know how to take (hold of) her,* for since "the value of commodities is the very opposite of the coarse materiality of their substance, not an atom of matter enters into its composition. Turn and examine a single commodity, by itself, as we will. Yet in so far as it remains an object of value, it seems impossible to grasp it" (ibid.). The value of a woman always escapes: black continent, hole in the symbolic, breach in discourse . . . It is only in the operation of exchange among women that something of this—something enigmatic, to be sure—can be felt. *Woman thus has value only in that she can be exchanged.* In the passage from one to the other, something else finally exists beside the possible utility of the "coarseness" of her body. But this value is not found, is not recaptured, in her. It is only her measurement against a third term that remains external to her, and that makes it possible to compare her with another woman, that permits her to have a relation to another commodity in terms of an equivalence that remains foreign to both.

Women-as-commodities are thus subject to a schism that divides them into the categories of usefulness and exchange value; into matter-body and an envelope that is precious but impenetrable, ungraspable, and not susceptible to appropriation by women themselves; into private use and social use.

In order to have a *relative value,* a commodity has to be confronted with another commodity that serves as its equivalent. Its value is never found to lie within itself. And the fact that it is worth more or less is not its own doing but comes from that to which it may be equivalent. Its value is *transcendent* to itself, *super-natural, ek-static.*

In other words, for the commodity, there is no mirror that copies it so that it may be at once itself and its "own" reflection. One commodity cannot be mirrored in another, as man is mirrored in his fellow man. For when we are dealing with commodities the self-same, mirrored, is not "its" own likeness, contains nothing of its properties, its qualities, its "skin and hair." The likeness here is only a measure expressing the *fabricated* character of the commodity, its trans-formation by man's (social, symbolic) "labor." The mirror that envelops and paralyzes the commodity specularizes, speculates (on) man's "labor." *Commodities, women, are a mirror of value of and for man.* In order to serve as such, they give up their bodies to men as the supporting material of specularization, of speculation. They yield to him their natural and social value as a locus of imprints, marks, and mirage of his activity.

Commodities among themselves are thus not equal, nor alike, nor different. They only become so when they are compared by and for man. And *the prosopopoeia of the relation of commodities among themselves is a projection* through which producers-exchangers make them reenact before their eyes their operations of specula(riza)tion. Forgetting that in order to reflect (oneself), to speculate (oneself), it is necessary to be a "subject," and that matter can serve as a support for speculation but cannot itself speculate in any way.

Thus, starting with the simplest relation of equivalence between commodities, starting with the possible exchange of women, the entire enigma of the money form—of the phallic function—is implied. That is, the appropriation-disappropriation by man, for man, of nature and its productive forces, insofar as a certain mirror now divides and travesties both nature and labor. Man endows the commodities he produces with a narcissism that blurs the seriousness of utility, of use. Desire, as soon as there is exchange, "perverts" need. But that perversion will be attributed to commodities and to their alleged relations. Whereas they can have no relationships except from the perspective of speculating third parties.

The economy of exchange—of desire—is man's business. For two reasons: the exchange takes place between masculine subjects, and it requires a *plus-value* added to the body of the commodity, a supplement which gives it a valuable form. That supplement will be found, Marx writes, in another commodity, whose use value becomes, from that point on, a standard of value.

But that surplus-value enjoyed by one of the commodities might vary: "just as many a man strutting about in a gorgeous uniform counts for more than when in mufti" (p. 60). Or just as "*A*, for instance, cannot be 'your majesty' to *B*, unless at the same time majesty in *B*'s eyes assume the bodily form of *A*, and, what is more, with every new father of the people, changes its features, hair, and many other things besides" (ibid.). Commodities—"things" produced—would thus have the respect due the uniform, majesty, paternal authority. And even God. "The fact that it is value, is made manifest by its equality with the coat, just as the sheep's nature of a Christian is shown in his resemblance to the Lamb of God" (ibid.).

Commodities thus share in the cult of the father, and never stop striving to resemble, to copy, the one who is his representative. It is from that resemblance, from that imitation of what represents paternal authority, that commodities draw their value—for men. But it is upon commodities that the producers-exchangers bring to bear this power play. "We see, then, all that our analysis of the value of commodities has already told us, is told us by the linen itself, so soon as it comes into communication with another commodity, the coat. Only it betrays its thoughts in that language with which alone it is familiar, the language of commodities. In order to tell us that its own value is created by labour in its abstract character of human labour, it says that the coat, in so far as it is worth as much as the linen, and therefore is value, consists of the same labour as the linen. In order to inform us that its sublime reality as value is not the same as its buckram body, it says that value has the appearance of a coat, and consequently that so far as the linen is value, it and the coat are as like as two peas. We may here remark, that the language of commodities has, besides Hebrew, many other more or less correct dialects. The German 'werthsein,' to be worth, for instance, expresses in a less striking manner than the Romance verbs 'valere,' 'valer,' 'valoir,' that the equating of commodity B to commodity A, is commodity A's own mode of expressing its value. Paris vaut bien une messe" (pp. 60–61).

So commodities speak. To be sure, mostly dialects and patois, languages hard for "subjects" to understand. The important thing is that they be preoccupied with their respective values, that their remarks confirm the exchangers' plans for them.

The body of a commodity thus becomes, for another such commodity, a mirror of its value. Contingent upon a bodily *supplement*. A supplement *opposed* to use value, a supplement representing the commodity's *super-natural* quality (an imprint that is purely social in nature), a supplement completely different from the body itself, and from its properties, a supplement that nevertheless exists only on condition that one commodity agrees to relate itself to another considered as equivalent: "For instance, one man is king only because other men stand in the relation of subjects to him" (p. 66, n. 1).

This supplement of equivalency translates concrete work into abstract work. In other words, in order to be able to incorporate itself into a mirror of value, it is necessary that the work itself reflect only its property of human labor: that the body of a commodity be nothing more than the materialization of an abstract human labor. That is, that it have no more body, matter, nature, but that it be objectivization, a crystallization as visible object, of man's activity.

In order to become equivalent, a commodity changes bodies. A super-natural, metaphysical origin is substituted for its material origin. Thus its body becomes a transparent body, *pure phenomenality of value*. But this transparency constitutes a supplement to the material opacity of the commodity.

Once again there is a schism between the two. Two sides, two poles, nature and society are divided, like the perceptible and the intelligible, matter and form, the empirical and the transcendental . . . The commodity, like the sign, suffers from metaphysical dichotomies. Its value, its truth, lies in the social element. But this social element is added on to its nature, to its matter, and the social subordinates it as a lesser value, indeed as nonvalue. Participation in society requires that the body submit itself to a specularization, a speculation, that transforms it into a value-bearing object, a standardized sign, an exchangeable signifier, a "likeness" with reference to an authoritative model. *A commodity—a woman—is divided into two irreconcilable "bodies":* her "natural" body and her socially valued, exchangeable body, which is a particularly mimetic expression of masculine values. No doubt these values also express "nature," that is, the expenditure of physical force. But this latter—essentially masculine, moreover—serves for the fabrication, the transformation, the technicization of natural productions. And it is this *super*-natural property that comes to constitute the value of the product. Analyzing value in this way, Marx exposes the meta-physical character of social operations.

The commodity is thus a dual entity as soon as its value comes to possess a phenomenal form of its own, distinct from its natural form: that of exchange value. And it never possesses this form if it is considered in isolation. A commodity has this phenomenal form added on to its nature only in relation to another commodity.

As among signs, value appears only when a relationship has been established. It remains the case that the establishment of relationships cannot be accomplished by the commodities themselves, but depends upon the operation of two exchangers. The exchange value of two signs, two commodities, two women, is a representation of the needs/desires of consumer-exchanger subjects: in no way is it the "property" of the signs/articles/women themselves. At the most, the commodities—or rather the relationships among them—are the material alibi for the desire for relations among men. To this end, the commodity is disinvested of its body and reclothed in a form that makes it suitable for exchange among men.

But, in this value-bearing form, the desire for that exchange, and the reflection of his own value and that of his fellow man that man seeks in it, are ek-stasized. In that suspension in the commodity of the relationship among men, producer-consumer-exchanger subjects are alienated. In order that they might "bear" and support that alienation, commodities for their part have always been dispossessed of their specific value. On this basis, one may affirm that the value of the commodity takes on *indifferently* any given form of use value. The price of the articles, in fact, no longer comes from *their* natural form, from *their* bodies, *their* language, but from the fact that they mirror the need/desire for exchanges among men. To do this, the commodity obviously cannot exist alone, but there is no such thing as a commodity, either, so long as there are not *at least two men* to make an exchange. In order for a product—a woman?—to have value, two men, at least, have to invest (in) her.

The general equivalent of a commodity no longer functions as a commodity itself. A preeminent mirror, transcending the world of merchandise, it guarantees the possibility of universal exchange among commodities. Each commodity may become equivalent to every other from the viewpoint of that sublime standard, but the fact that the judgment of their value depends upon some transcendental element renders them provisionally incapable of being directly exchanged for each other. They are exchanged by means of the general equivalent—as Christians love each other in God, to borrow a theological metaphor dear to Marx.

That ek-static reference separates them radically from each other. *An abstract and universal value preserves them from use and exchange among themselves.* They are, as it were, transformed into value-invested idealities. Their concrete forms, their specific qualities, and all the possibilities of "real" relations with them or among them are reduced to their common character as products of man's labor and desire.

We must emphasize also that *the general equivalent,* since it is no longer a commodity, *is no longer useful. The standard as such is exempt from use.*

Though a commodity may at first sight appear to be "a very trivial thing, and easily understood, . . . it is, in reality, a very queer thing, abounding in metaphysical subtleties and theological niceties" (p. 81). No doubt, "so far as it is a value in use, there is nothing mysterious about it. . . . But, so soon as [a wooden table, for example] steps forth as a commodity, it is changed into something transcendent. It not only stands with its feet on the ground, but, in relation to all other commodities, it stands on its head, and evolves out of its wooden brain grotesque ideas, far more wonderful than 'table-turning' ever was" (pp. 81–82).

"The mystical character of commodities does not originate, therefore, in their use value. Just as little does it proceed from the nature of the determining factors of value. For, in the first place, however varied the useful kinds of labour, or productive activities, may be, it is a physiological fact, that they are functions of the human organism" (p. 82), which, for Marx, does not seem to constitute a mystery in any way . . . The material contribution and support of bodies in societal operations pose no problems for him, except as production and expenditure of energy.

Where, then, does the enigmatic character of the product of labor come from, as soon as this product takes on the form of a commodity? It comes, obviously, from that form itself. *Then where does the enigmatic character of women come from?* Or even that of their supposed relations among themselves? Obviously, from the "form" of the needs/desires of man, needs/desires that women bring to light although men do not recognize them in that form. That form, those women, are always enveloped, veiled.

In any case, "the existence of things *qua* commodities, and the value relation between the products of labour which stamps them as commodities, have absolutely no connection with their physical properties and with the material relations arising therefrom. [With commodities] it is a definite social relation between men, that assumes, in their eyes, the fantastic form of a relation between things" (p. 83). *This phenomenon has no analogy except in the religious world.* "In that world the productions of the human brain appear as independent beings endowed with life, and entering into relation both with one another and the human race. So it is in the world of commodities with the products of men's hands" (ibid.). Hence the fetishism attached to these products of labor as soon as they present themselves as commodities.

Hence *women's role as fetish-objects,* inasmuch as, in exchanges, they are the manifestation and the circulation of a power of the Phallus, establishing relationships of men with each other?

*

Hence the following remarks:

On value.

It represents the equivalent of labor force, of an expenditure of energy, of toil. In order to be measured, these latter must be *abstracted* from all immediately natural qualities, from any concrete individual. A process of generalization and of universalization imposes itself in the operation of social exchanges. Hence the reduction of man to a "concept"—that of his labor force—and the reduction of his product to an "object," the visible, material correlative of that concept.

The characteristics of "sexual pleasure" corresponding to such a social state are thus the following: its productivity, but one that is necessarily laborious, even painful; its abstract form; its need/desire to crystallize in a transcendental element of wealth the standard of all value; its need for a material support where the relation of appropriation to and of that standard is measured; its exchange relationships—always rivalrous—among men alone, and so on.

Are not these modalities the ones that might define the economy of (so-called) *masculine sexuality?* And is libido not another name for the abstraction of "energy" in a productive power? For the work of nature? Another name for the desire to accumulate goods? Another name for the subordination of the specific qualities of bodies to a—neutral?—power that aims above all to transform them in order to possess them? Does pleasure, for masculine sexuality, consist in anything other than the appropriation of nature, in the desire to make it (re)produce, and in exchanges of its/these products with other members of society? An essentially *economic* pleasure.

Thus the following question: *what needs/desires of (so-called) masculine sexuality have presided over the evolution of a certain social order,* from its primitive form, private property, to its developed form, capital? But also: *to what extent are these needs/desires the effect of a social mechanism,* in part autonomous, that produces them as such?

On the status of women in such a social order.

What makes such an order possible, what assures its foundation, is thus *the exchange of women.* The circulation of women among men is what establishes the operations of society, at least of patriarchal society. Whose presuppositions include the following: the appropriation of nature by man; the transformation of nature according to "human" criteria, defined by men alone; the submission of nature to labor and technology; the reduction of its material, corporeal, perceptible qualities to man's practical concrete activity; the equality of women among themselves, but in terms of laws of equivalence that remain external to them; the constitution of women as "objects" that emblematize the materialization of relations among men, and so on.

In such a social order, women thus represent a natural value and a social value. Their "development" lies in the passage from one to the other. But this passage never takes place simply.

As mother, woman remains on the side of (re)productive *nature* and, because of this, man can never fully transcend his relation to the "natural." His social existence, his economic structures and his sexuality are always tied to the work of nature: these structures thus always remain at the level of the earliest appropriation, that of the constitution of nature as landed property, and of the earliest labor, which is agricultural. But this relationship to productive nature, an insurmountable one, has to be denied so that relations among men may prevail. This means that mothers, reproductive instruments marked with the name of the father and enclosed in his house, must be private property, excluded from exchange. The *incest taboo* represents this refusal to allow productive nature to enter into exchanges among men. As both natural value and use value, mothers cannot circulate in the form of commodities without threatening the very existence of the social order. Mothers are essential to its (re)production (particularly inasmuch as they are [re]productive of children and of the labor force: through maternity, child-rearing, and domestic maintenance in general). Their responsibility is to maintain the social order without intervening so as to change it. Their products are legal tender in that order, moreover, only if they are marked with the name of the father, only if they are recognized within his law: that is, only insofar as they are appropriated by him. Society is the place where man engenders himself, where man produces himself as man, where man is born into "human," "super-natural" existence.

The virginal woman, on the other hand, is pure exchange value. She is nothing but the possibility, the place, the sign of relations among men. In and of herself, she does not exist: she is a simple envelope veiling what is really at stake in social exchange. In this sense, her natural body disappears into its representative function. *Red blood* remains on the mother's side, but it has no price, as such, in the social order; woman, for her part, as medium of exchange, is no longer anything but *semblance.* The ritualized passage from woman to mother is accomplished by the *violation of an envelope:* the hymen, which has taken on the value of *taboo,* the taboo of virginity. Once deflowered, woman is relegated to the status of use value, to her entrapment in private property; she is removed from exchange among men.

The *prostitute* remains to be considered. Explicitly condemned by the social order, she is implicitly tolerated. No doubt because the break between usage and exchange is, in her case, less clear-cut? In her case, the qualities of woman's body are "useful." However, these qualities have "value" only because they have already been appropriated by a man, and because they serve as the locus of relations—hidden ones—between men. Prostitution amounts to *usage that is exchanged.* Usage that is not merely potential: it has already been realized. The woman's body is valuable because it has already been used. In the extreme case, the more it has served, the more it is worth. Not because its natural assets have been put to use this way, but, on the contrary, because its nature has been "used up," and has become once again no more than a vehicle for relations among men.

Mother, virgin, prostitute: these are the social roles imposed on women. The characteristics of (so-called) feminine sexuality derive from them: the valorization of reproduction and nursing; faithfulness; modesty, ignorance of and even lack of interest in sexual pleasure; a passive acceptance of men's "activity"; seductiveness, in order to arouse the consumers' desire while offering herself as its material support without getting pleasure herself . . . *Neither as mother nor as virgin nor as prostitute has woman any right to her own pleasure.*

Of course the theoreticians of sexuality are sometimes astonished by women's frigidity. But, according to them, this frigidity is explained more by an impotence inherent to feminine "nature" than by the submission of that nature to a certain type of society. However, *what is required of a "normal" feminine sexuality is oddly evocative of the characteristics of the status of a commodity.* With references to and rejections of the "natural"—physiological and organic nature, and so on—that are equally ambiguous.

And, in addition:

—just as nature has to be subjected to man in order to become a commodity, so, it appears, does "the development of a normal woman." A development that amounts, for the feminine, to subordination to the forms and laws of masculine activity. The rejection of the mother—imputed to woman—would find its "cause" here;

—just as, in commodities, natural utility is overridden by the exchange function, so the properties of a woman's body have to be suppressed and subordinated to the exigencies of its transformation into an object of circulation among men;

—just as a commodity has no mirror it can use to reflect itself, so woman serves as reflection, as image of and for man, but lacks specific qualities of her own. Her value-invested form amounts to what man inscribes in and on its matter: that is, her body;

—just as commodities cannot make exchanges among themselves without the intervention of a subject that measures them against a standard, so it is with women. Distinguished, divided, separated, classified as like and unlike, according to whether they have been judged exchangeable. In themselves, among themselves, they are amorphous and confused: natural body, maternal body, doubtless useful to the consumer, but without any possible identity or communicable value;

—just as commodities, despite their resistance, become more or less autonomous repositories for the value of human work, so, as mirrors of and for man, women more or less unwittingly come to represent the danger of a disappropriation of masculine power: the phallic mirage;

—just as a commodity finds the expression of its value in an equivalent—in the last analysis, a general one—that necessarily remains external to it, so woman derives her price from her relation to the male sex, constituted as a transcendental value: the phallus. And indeed the enigma of "value" lies in the most elementary relation among commodities. Among women. For, uprooted from their "nature," they no longer relate to each other except in terms of what they represent in men's desire, and according to the "forms" that this imposes upon them. Among themselves, they are separated by his speculations.

This means that the division of "labor"—sexual labor in particular—requires that woman maintain in her own body the material substratum of the object of desire, but that she herself never have access to desire. The economy of desire—of exchange—is man's business. And that economy subjects women to a schism that is necessary to symbolic operations: red blood/semblance; body/value-invested envelope; matter/medium of exchange; (re)productive nature/fabricated femininity . . . That schism—characteristic of all speaking nature, someone will surely object—is experienced by women without any possible profit to them. And without any way for them to transcend it. They are not even "conscious" of it. The symbolic system that cuts them in two this way is in no way appropriate to them. In them, "semblance" remains external, foreign to "nature." *Socially,* they are "objects" for and among men and furthermore they cannot do anything but mimic a "language" that they have not produced; *naturally,* they remain amorphous, suffering from drives without any possible representatives or representations. For them, the transformation of the natural into the social does not take place, except to the extent that they function as components of private property, or as commodities.

Characteristics of this social order

This type of social system can be interpreted as *the practical realization of the meta-physical.* As the *practical destiny* of the meta-physical, it would also represent its *most fully realized form.* Operating in such a way, moreover, that subjects themselves, being implicated in it through and through, being produced in it as concepts, would lack the means to analyze it. Except in an after-the-fact way whose delays are yet to be fully measured . . .

This practical realization of the meta-physical has as its founding operation the appropriation of woman's body by the father or his substitutes. It is marked by women's submission to a system of general equivalents, the proper name representing the father's monopoly of power. It is from this standardization that women receive their value, as they pass from the state of nature to the status of social object. This trans-formation of women's bodies into use values and exchange values inaugurates the symbolic order. But that order depends upon a *nearly pure added value.* Women, animals endowed with speech like men, assure the possibility of the use and circulation of the symbolic without being recipients of it. Their nonaccess to the symbolic is what has established the social order. Putting men in touch with each other, in relations among themselves, women only fulfill this role by relinquishing their right to speech and even to animality. No longer in the natural order, not yet in the social order that they nonetheless maintain, women are the symptom of the exploitation of individuals by a society that remunerates them only partially, or even not at all, for their "work." Unless subordination to a system that utilizes you and oppresses you should be considered as sufficient compensation . . . ? Unless the fact that women are branded with the proper name—of the "father"—should be viewed as the symbolic payment awarded them for sustaining the social order with their bodies?

But by submitting women's bodies to a general equivalent, to a transcendent, super-natural value, men have drawn the social structure into an ever greater process of abstraction, to the point where they themselves are produced in it as pure concepts: having surmounted all their "perceptible" qualities and individual differences, they are finally reduced to the average productivity of their labor. The power of this practical economy of the meta-physical comes from the fact that "physiological" energy is transformed into abstract value without the mediation of an intelligible elaboration. No individual subject can be credited any longer with bringing about this transformation. It is only after the fact that the subject might possibly be able to analyze his determination as such by the social structure. And even then it is not certain that his love of gold would not make him give up everything else before he would renounce the cult of this fetish. "The saver thus sacrifices to this fetish all the penchants of his flesh. No one takes the gospel of renunciation more seriously than he."

Fortunately—if we may say so—women/commodities would remain, as simple "objects" of transaction among men. Their situation of specific exploitation in exchange operations—sexual exchange, and economic, social, and cultural exchanges in general—might lead them to offer a new critique of the political economy." *A critique that would no longer avoid that of discourse, and more generally of the symbolic system, in which it is realized.* Which would lead to interpreting in a different way the impact of symbolic social labor in the analysis of relations of production.

For, without the exploitation of women, what would become of the social order? What modifications would it undergo if women left behind their condition as commodities—subject to being produced, consumed, valorized, circulated, and so on, by men alone—and took part in elaborating and carrying out exchanges? Not by reproducing, by copying, the "phallocratic" models that have the force of law today, but by socializing in a different way the relation to nature, matter, the body, language, and desire.

9

Commodities among Themselves

The exchanges upon which patriarchal societies are based take place exclusively among men. Women, signs, commodities, and currency always pass from one man to another; if it were otherwise, we are told, the social order would fall back upon incestuous and exclusively endogamous ties that would paralyze all commerce. Thus the labor force and its products, including those of mother earth, are the object of transactions among men and men alone. This means that the *very possibility of a sociocultural order requires homosexuality* as its organizing principle. Heterosexuality is nothing but the assignment of economic roles: there are producer subjects and agents of exchange (male) on the one hand, productive earth and commodities (female) on the other.

Culture, at least in its patriarchal form, thus effectively prohibits any return to *red blood,* including that of the sexual arena. *In consequence, the ruling power is pretense, or sham, which still fails to recognize its own endogamies.* For in this culture the only sex, the only sexes, are those needed to keep relationships among men running smoothly.

Why is masculine homosexuality considered exceptional, then, when in fact the economy as a whole is based upon it? Why are homosexuals ostracized, when society postulates homosexuality? Unless it is because the *"incest" involved in homosexuality has to remain in the realm of pretense.*

This text was originally published as "Des marchandises entre elles," in *La quinzaine littéraire,* no. 215 (August 1975). English translation: "Commodities on Their Own," trans. Claudia Reeder, in *New French Feminisms,* ed. Elaine Marks and Isabelle de Courtivron (New York, 1981), pp. 107–110.

Consider the exemplary case of *father-son relationships,* which guarantee the transmission of patriarchal power and its laws, its discourse, its social structures. These relations, which are in effect everywhere, cannot be eradicated through the abolition of the family or of monogamous reproduction, nor can they openly display the pederastic love in which they are grounded. They cannot be put into practice at all, except in language, without provoking a general crisis, without bringing one sort of symbolic system to an end.

The "other" homosexual relations, masculine ones, are just as subversive, so they too are forbidden. *Because they openly interpret the law according to which society operates,* they threaten in fact to shift the horizon of that law. Besides, they challenge the nature, status, and "exogamic" necessity of the product of exchange. By short-circuiting the mechanisms of commerce, might they also expose what is really at stake? Furthermore, they might lower the sublime value of the standard, the yardstick. Once the penis itself becomes merely a means to pleasure, pleasure among men, *the phallus loses its power.* Sexual pleasure, we are told, is best left to those creatures who are ill-suited for the seriousness of symbolic rules, namely, women.

Exchanges and relationships, always among men, would thus be *both required and forbidden by law.* There is a price to pay for being the agents of exchange: male subjects have to give up the possibility of serving as commodities themselves.

Thus all economic organization is homosexual. That of desire as well, even the desire for women. Woman exists only as an occasion for mediation, transaction, transition, transference, between man and his fellow man, indeed between man and himself.

*

Considering that the peculiar status of what is called heterosexuality has managed, and is still managing, to escape notice, *how can relationships among women be accounted for in this system of exchange?* Except by the assertion that as soon as she desires (herself), as soon as she speaks (expresses herself, to herself), a woman is a man. As soon as she has any relationship with another woman, she is homosexual, and therefore masculine.

Freud makes this clear in his analyses of female homosexuality.[1]

A woman chooses homosexuality only by virtue of a "masculinity complex" (p. 169). Whether this complex is a "direct and unchanged continuation of an infantile fixation" (p. 168) or a regression toward an earlier "masculinity complex," *it is only as a man that the female homosexual can desire a woman who reminds her of a man.* That is why women in homosexual relationships can play the roles of mother and child or husband and wife, without distinction.

The mother stands for phallic power; the child is always a little boy; the husband is a father-man. And the woman? She "doesn't exist." She adopts the disguise that she is told to put on. She acts out the role that is imposed on her. The only thing really required of her is that she *keep intact the circulation of pretense by enveloping herself in femininity.* Hence the fault, the infraction, the misconduct, and the challenge that female homosexuality entails. The problem can be minimized if female homosexuality is regarded merely as an imitation of male behavior.

So, "in her behaviour towards her love-object," the female homosexual, Freud's at any rate, "throughout assumed the masculine part" (p. 154); not only did she choose a "feminine love-object," but she also "developed a masculine attitude towards that object" (p. 154). She "changed into a man and took her [phallic] mother in place of her father as the object of her

[1]See Sigmund Freud, "The Psychogenesis of a Case of Homosexuality in a Woman," in *Standard Edition of the Complete Works of Sigmund Freud,* ed. James Strachey, 24 vols. (London, 1953–1974), *18:*147–171.

love" (p. 158), but her fixation on "the lady" was explained all the same by the fact that "her lady's slender figure, severe beauty and downright manner reminded her of the brother who was a little older than herself" (p. 156).

How can we account for this "perversion" of the sexual function assigned to a "normal" woman? Our psychoanalyst's interpretation encounters some difficulty here. The phenomenon of female homosexuality appears so foreign to his "theory," to his (cultural) imaginary, that it cannot help but be "neglected by psychoanalytic research" (p. 147).

Thus to avoid a serious challenge to his new science, he has to refer this awkward problem back to an anatomo-physiological cause: "of course the constitutional factor is undoubtedly of decisive importance." And Freud is on the lookout for anatomical indications that would account for the homosexuality—the *masculine* homosexuality—of his "patient." "Certainly there was no obvious deviation from the feminine physical type," she was "beautiful and well-made," and presented no "menstrual disturbance," but she had, "it is true, her father's tall figure, and her facial features were sharp rather than soft and girlish, traits which might be regarded as indicating a physical masculinity," and in addition "some of her intellectual attributes also could be connected with masculinity" (p. 154). But . . . "the psycho-analyst customarily forgoes a thorough physical examination of his patients in certain cases" (p. 154).

If he had not refrained from looking, what might Freud have discovered as anatomical proof of the homosexuality, the *masculine* homosexuality, of his "patient"? What would his desire, his inadmissible desire, for *disguises* have led him to "see"? To cover up all those fantasies with a still anatomo-physiological objectivity, he merely mentions "probably hermaphroditic ovaries" (p. 172). And finally he dismisses the girl, advising her parents that "if they set store by the therapeutic procedure it should be continued by a woman doctor" (p. 164).

Not a word has been said here about *feminine* homosexuality. Neither the girl's nor Freud's. Indeed, the "patient" seemed completely indifferent to the treatment process, although her "intellectual participation" was considerable. *Perhaps the only transference was Freud's?* A negative transference, as they say. Or denegational. For how could he possibly have identified himself with a "lady" . . . who moreover was "'of bad repute' sexually," a "*cocotte,*" someone who "lived simply by giving her bodily favours" (p. 161)? How could his "superego" have permitted him to be "quite simply" a woman? Still, that would have been the only way to avoid blocking his "patient's" transference.

So female homosexuality has eluded psychoanalysis. Which is not to say that Freud's description is simply incorrect. The dominant sociocultural economy leaves female homosexuals only a choice between a sort of *animality* that Freud seems to overlook and *the imitation of male models.* In this economy any interplay of desire among women's bodies, women's organs, women's language is inconceivable.

And yet female homosexuality does exist. But it is recognized only to the extent that it is *prostituted to man's fantasies.* Commodities can only enter into relationships under the watchful eyes of their "guardians." It is out of the question for them to go to "market" on their own, enjoy their own worth among themselves, speak to each other, desire each other, free from the control of seller-buyer-consumer subjects. And the interests of businessmen require that commodities relate to each other as rivals.

*

But what if these "commodities" refused to go to "market"? What if they maintained "another" kind of commerce, among themselves?

Exchanges without identifiable terms, without accounts, without end . . . Without additions and accumulations, one plus one, woman after woman . . . Without sequence or number. Without standard or yardstick. *Red blood* and *sham* would no longer be differentiated by deceptive envelopes concealing their worth. Use and exchange would be indistinguishable. The greatest value would be at the same time the least kept in reserve. Nature's resources would be expended without depletion, exchanged without labor, freely given, exempt from masculine transactions: enjoyment without a fee, well-being without pain, pleasure without possession. As for all the strategies and savings, the appropriations tantamount to theft and rape, the laborious accumulation of capital, how ironic all that would be.

Utopia? Perhaps. Unless this mode of exchange has undermined the order of commerce from the beginning—while the *necessity of keeping incest in the realm of pure pretense* has stood in the way of a certain economy of abundance.

10

"Frenchwomen," Stop Trying

In the pornographic scene, there is nothing for me to say. I am to listen and repeat the teaching that a libertine master is addressing to a young foreigner—male or female?—just emerging from ignorance, and I am to give myself over, voluptuously, to his practices. Or to those of his acolytes, as Socratic preference demands. At most, I am supposed to display my enthusiasm: "Yes, yes, yes . . ." "To be sure." "Obviously." "Of course." "How could it be otherwise?" "Who could disagree with that?" and other sounds, less clearly articulated, which prove to the master that I am ecstatic about what he knows how to say or do.

That is indeed the case: I am beside myself. Overcome. Overtaken (which also means "beaten"). From this point on—he professes—I am to enter into my pleasure. First I have to lose consciousness—and existence?—through the theoretical and practical power of his language.

If I could somehow remain outside the scene and resist or survive the grip of this sovereign authority I would risk asking the libertine master a few questions. Which he would not hear. Or which he would take as proof of infidelity to what he calls "my nature." Better yet, as an effect of censorship. Doesn't he need that, after all, to keep his pleasures coming? There's no doubt, in any case, that he'll evade my questioning in the name of some legalism. For he is assuredly a born legislator.

This text was originally published as "'Françaises,' ne faites plus un effort . . ." in *La quinzaine littéraire,* no. 238 (August 1976).

Questions for the pornographers

—The pornographic scene can be viewed paradigmatically as the initiation and training of a woman who is and continues to be virginal with respect to the pleasure that some man purports to be teaching her. Thus to all appearances the woman has the leading role; she is the major attraction. She must be suitably young and beautiful.

To whom is this woman being shown, in her body and her pleasure? For whom is man's sex represented? Isn't it, finally, to another man that the statements and performances of the professor of immorality are addressed? In a relationship established between (at least) two men, the ignorant young woman is the *mediation prescribed by society.* The woman is all the more in the foreground because the scene is played out between men. In such a system, what is the *function of woman's sexual pleasure?*

—Furthermore, *is woman's pleasure even at issue?* That a woman has one, two, ten or twenty orgasms, to the point of complete exhaustion (*lassata sed non satiata?*), does not mean that she takes pleasure in her pleasure. Those orgasms are necessary as a demonstration of masculine power. They signify the success—men think—of their sexual domination of women. They are *proof that the techniques for pleasure men have elaborated are valid, that man is the uncontested master of the means of production of pleasure.* Women are there as witnesses. Their training is designed to subject them to an exclusively phallocratic sexual economy. Novices succumb completely to their wide-eyed appetite for erection, violent penetration, repeated blows and injuries. Full-fledged female libertines speak and act like phallocrats: they seduce, suck, screw, strike, even slaughter those weaker than themselves, like the strong men they are.

Token women, they're called. For the techniques for pleasure applied in pornography have hardly been suited—at least up to now?—for women's pleasure. The obsession with erection and ejaculation, the exaggerated importance of penis size, the stereotyped poverty of gesture, the reduction of the body to a mere surface to be broken through or punctured, violence and rape . . . all these perhaps bring woman forcibly to sexual pleasure (women are gifted . . .), but what sort of pleasure is it?

And if women stay *mute* about their pleasure, if they *remain ignorant,* how can anyone be surprised? "Nature," subjected to uniquely masculine modes of production, takes her pleasure through women, so long as they submit to it in total ignorance. The (male) libertine is a little better informed, thanks to women's pleasure, and gets his premium in sexual pleasure from that knowledge.

—He even incites women to enjoy each other sexually—under his watchful eye, of course. He must not allow any possibility of sexual staging to escape him. So long as he is the organizer, anything goes. The question remains: in what way does he see what goes on between women? In other words: *do women who are "among-themselves-under-his-watchful-eye" behave as they do among themselves?*

—For example: the libertine loves blood. At least the blood that flows according to his own techniques. For whatever form his libertinage may take, however he may flout all (?) prohibitions, *menstrual blood generally remains taboo.* Excrement may be all right, but menstrual flow, no . . .

Might he be unwittingly censuring some aspect of "nature"? Why blood, specifically? Whose blood? And why are women subject to these prohibitory systems? Don't they want to make love, really, during their periods? Do they share—but through the power of what suggestions?—in the horror of their own blood? Is it this induced repulsion that makes them hate their mother's sex?

—More blood . . .Passivity, and more specifically penetration, are always represented as painful. Pain as a necessary component of pleasure: that of the male who penetrates, that of the male or female who is penetrated. *What fantasy of a closed, solid, virginal body to be forced open* underlies such a representation, and such a practice, of sexuality? In this view, the body's pleasure always results from a forced entry—preferably bloody—into an *enclosure.* A *property?* By whom, for whom, is that property constituted? Which man (or men) does this quasi crime against private property concern? Even though it is most often committed on women's bodies.

—The libertine, at any rate, is usually well supplied with money, language, and techniques. Is it by virtue of this appropriation of wealth and instruments of production that he seduces—buys—women and children, those who are "poorest," and that he compels them to sexual pleasure? The question arises once again: what pleasure? Is it perhaps because he is not obliged to work that he has all the time he needs to perfect his knowledge of pleasure?

Might that be his proper work? *How is such work articulated with the world of work in general?* Isn't today's pornographer a civil servant devoted to questions of public health?

In fact, the pornographic scene—tacitly or explicitly encouraged by the powers of the State—works as a space carefully partioned off for "discharge" and "pollution" ad nauseum. A place where human machines can go for periodical cleaning, where they can be emptied of their desires and possible sexual superfluities. Human bodies, purged of their potential excesses, can return to the rut, to their familiar slot in the circuits of work, society, or family. Everything will go along properly until the next time.

—The next time? The pornographic scene is *indefinitely repetitive.* It never stops. It always has to start over. One more time. And another. The alibi of pleasure covers the need for endless reiteration.

What is it that eludes pleasure this way, making the repetition compulsion so tyrannical? Leaving a categorical imperative to dictate the pursuit of some pleasure that is never used up? For physical exhaustion alone determines the stopping-point of the scene, not the attainment of a more exhaustive pleasure. Such a pleasure in fact becomes increasingly rare and costly: the master requires more and more of it for his enjoyment. Pornography is the *reign of the series.* One more time, one more "victim," one more blow, one more death . . .

—But within a closed circuit, a circumscribed space and time. The scene unfailingly produces satiation and boredom. The only "way out" lies in the quantitative dimension. Or else death is the outlet for this endless cycle. *Where does this prescription for monotony come from?* Isn't libertinage also determined by a superego that is as cruel in action as it is automatic? In this mechanization of pleasure, sexualized bodies come to be immolated in a sacrifice that best succeeds when it achieves black-out (in) death.

Hence another question: for man, must the abundance, real or fantasmatic, on which pornographic seduction basically depends *go on forever seeking expiation through loss?* Must "more than" always end up as "less than"? Must accumulation end in discharge, disposal? Until the reserves are exhausted? And then it begins again. On the horizon of the pornographic scene is there perhaps a lingering fascination with loss? Is man admitting his incapacity to enjoy wealth? To enjoy nature? *What all-powerful and implacably persecuting myth dominates the structure of this sexual scenography?*

One could ask pornographers many other questions. Without even confronting the issue of whether one is "for" or "against" their practices. After all, it is better for the sexuality that underlies our social order to be exercised openly than for it to prescribe that social order from the hiding-place of its repressions. Perhaps if the phallocracy that reigns everywhere is put unblushingly on display, a different sexual economy may become possible? Pornography as "catharsis" of the phallic empire? As the unmasking of women's sexual subjection?

Women out of the bedroom

Women, stop trying. You have been taught that you were property, private or public, belonging to one man or all. To family, tribe, State, even a Republic. That therein lay your pleasure. And that, unless you gave in to man's, or men's, desires, you would not know sexual pleasure. That pleasure was, for you, always tied to pain, but that such was your nature. If you disobeyed, you were the cause of your own unhappiness.

But, curiously enough, your nature has always been defined by men, and men alone. Your eternal instructors, in social science, religion, or sex. Your moral or immoral teachers. They are the ones who have taught you your needs or desires. You haven't yet had a word to say on the subject.

So ask yourselves just what "nature" is speaking along their theoretical or practical lines. And if you find yourselves attracted by something other than what *their* laws, rules, and rituals prescribe, realize that—perhaps—you have come across *your* "nature."

Don't even go looking for that alibi. Do what comes to mind, do what you like: without "reasons," without "valid motives," without "justification." You don't have to raise your impulses to the lofty status of categorical imperatives: neither for your own benefit nor for anybody else's. Your impulses may change; they may or may not coincide with those of some other, man or woman. Today, not tomorrow. Don't force yourselves to repeat, don't congeal your dreams or desires in unique and definitive representations. You have so many continents to explore that if you set up borders for yourselves you won't be able to "enjoy" all of your own "nature."

11

When Our Lips Speak Together

If we keep on speaking the same language together, we're going to reproduce the same history. Begin the same old stories all over again. Don't you think so? Listen: all round us, men and women sound just the same. The same discussions, the same arguments, the same scenes. The same attractions and separations. The same difficulties, the same impossibility of making connections. The same . . . Same . . . Always the same.

If we keep on speaking sameness, if we speak to each other as men have been doing for centuries, as we have been taught to speak, we'll miss each other, fail ourselves. Again . . . Words will pass through our bodies, above our heads. They'll vanish, and we'll be lost. Far off, up high. Absent from ourselves: we'll be spoken machines, speaking machines. Enveloped in proper skins, but not our own. Withdrawn into proper names, violated by them. Not yours, not mine. We don't have any. We change names as men exchange us, as they use us, use us up. It would be frivolous of us, exchanged by them, to be so changeable.

How can I touch you if you're not there? Your blood has become their meaning. They can speak to each other, and about us. But what about us? Come out of their language. Try to go back through the names they've given you. I'll wait for you,

This text was originally published as "Quand nos lèvres se parlent," in *Cahiers du Grif,* no. 12. English translation: "When Our Lips Speak Together," trans. Carolyn Burke, in *Signs,* 6:1 (Fall 1980), 69–79.

I'm waiting for myself. Come back. It's not so hard. You stay here, and you won't be absorbed into familiar scenes, worn-out phrases, routine gestures. Into bodies already encoded within a system. Try to pay attention to yourself. To me. Without letting convention, or habit, distract you.

For example: "I love you" is addressed by convention or habit to an enigma—an other. An other body, an other sex. I love you: I don't quite know who, or what. "I love" flows away, is buried, drowned, burned, lost in a void. We'll have to wait for the return of "I love." Perhaps a long time, perhaps forever. Where has "I love" gone? What has become of me? "I love" lies in wait for the other. Has he swallowed me up? Spat me out? Taken me? Left me? Locked me up? Thrown me out? What's he like now? No longer (like) me? When he tells me "I love you," is he giving me back? Or is he giving himself in that form? His? Mine? The same? Another? But then where am I, what have I become?

When you say I love you—staying right here, close to you, close to me—you're saying I love myself. You don't need to wait for it to be given back; neither do I. We don't owe each other anything. That "I love you" is neither gift nor debt. You "give" me nothing when you touch yourself, touch me, when you touch yourself again through me. You don't give yourself. What would I do with you, with myself, wrapped up like a gift? You keep our selves to the extent that you share us. You find our selves to the extent that you trust us. Alternatives, oppositions, choices, bargains like these have no business between us. Unless we restage their commerce, and remain within their order. Where "we" has no place.

I love you: body shared, undivided. Neither you nor I severed. There is no need for blood shed, between us. No need for a wound to remind us that blood exists. It flows within us, from us. Blood is familiar, close. You are all red. And so very white. Both at once. You don't become red by losing your candid whiteness. You are white because you have remained close to blood. White and red at once, we give birth to all the colors: pinks, browns, blonds, greens, blues . . . For this whiteness is no sham. It is not dead blood, black blood. Sham is black. It absorbs everything, closed in on itself, trying to come back to life. Trying in vain . . . Whereas red's whiteness takes nothing away. Luminous, without autarchy, it gives back as much as it receives.

We are luminous. Neither one nor two. I've never known how to count. Up to you. In their calculations, we make two. Really, two? Doesn't that make you laugh? An odd sort of two. And yet not one. Especially not one. Let's leave *one* to them: their oneness, with its prerogatives, its domination, its solipsism: like the sun's. And the strange way they divide up their couples, with the other as the image of the one. Only an image. So any move toward the other means turning back to the attraction of one's own mirage. A (scarcely) living mirror, she/it is frozen, mute. More lifelike. The ebb and flow of our lives spent in the exhausting labor of copying, miming. Dedicated to reproducing—that sameness in which we have remained for centuries, as the other.

But how can I put "I love you" differently? I love you, my indifferent one? That still means yielding to their language. They've left us only lacks, deficiencies, to designate ourselves. They've left us their negative(s). We ought to be—that's already going too far—indifferent.

Indifferent one, keep still. When you stir, you disturb their order. You upset everything. You break the circle of their habits, the circularity of their exchanges, their knowledge, their desire. Their world. Indifferent one, you mustn't move, or be moved, unless they call you. If they say "come," then you may go ahead. Barely. Adapting yourself to whatever need they have, or don't have, for the presence of their own image. One step, or two. No more. No exuberance. No turbulence. Otherwise you'll smash everything. The ice, the mirror. Their earth, their mother. And what about your life? You must pretend to receive it from them. You're an indifferent, insignificant little receptacle, subject to their demands alone.

So they think we're indifferent. Doesn't that make you laugh? At least for a moment, here and now? *We* are *indifferent?* (If you keep on laughing that way, we'll never be able to talk to each other. We'll remain absorbed in their words, violated by them. So let's try to take back some part of our mouth to speak with.) Not different; that's right. Still . . . No, that would be too easy. And that "not" still keeps us separate so we can be compared. Disconnected that way, no more "us"? Are we alike? If you like. It's a little abstract. I don't quite understand "alike." Do you? Alike in whose eyes? in what terms? by what standard? with reference to what third? I'm touching you, that's quite enough to let me know that you are my body.

I love you: our two lips cannot separate to let just *one* word pass. A single word that would say "you," or "me." Or "equals"; she who loves, she who is loved. Closed and open, neither ever excluding the other, they say they both love each other. Together. To produce a single precise word, they would have to stay apart. Definitely parted. Kept at a distance, separated by *one word*.

But where would that word come from? Perfectly correct, closed up tight, wrapped around its meaning. Without any opening, any fault. "You." "Me." You may laugh . . . Closed and faultless, it is no longer you or me. Without lips, there is no more "us." The unity, the truth, the propriety of words comes from their lack of lips, their forgetting of lips. Words are mute, when they are uttered once and for all. Neatly wrapped up so that their meaning—their blood—won't escape. Like the children of men? Not ours. And besides, do we need, or want, children? What for? Here and now, we are close. Men and women have children to embody their closeness, their distance. But we?

I love you, childhood. I love you who are neither mother (forgive me, mother, I prefer a woman) nor sister. Neither daughter nor son. I love you—and where I love you, what do I care about the lineage of our fathers, or their desire for reproductions of men? Or their genealogical institutions? What need have I for husband or wife, for family, persona, role, function? Let's leave all those to men's reproductive laws. I love you, your body, here and now. I/you touch you/me, that's quite enough for us to feel alive.

Open your lips; don't open them simply. I don't open them simply. We—you/I—are neither open nor closed. We never separate simply: *a single word* cannot be pronounced, produced, uttered by our mouths. Between our lips, yours and mine, several voices, several ways of speaking resound endlessly, back and forth. One is never separable from the other. You/I: we are always several at once. And how could one dominate the other? impose her voice, her tone, her meaning? One cannot be distinquished from the other; which does not mean that they are indistinct. You don't understand a thing? No more than they understand you.

Speak, all the same. It's our good fortune that your language isn't formed of a single thread, a single strand or pattern. It comes from everywhere at once. You touch me all over at the same time. In all senses. Why only one song, one speech, one text at at time? To seduce, to satisfy, to fill one of my "holes"? With you, I don't have any. We are not lacks, voids awaiting sustenance, plenitude, fulfillment from the other. By our lips we are women: this does not mean that we are focused on consuming, consummation, fulfillment.

Kiss me. Two lips kissing two lips: openness is ours again. Our "world." And the passage from the inside out, from the outside in, the passage between us, is limitless. Without end. No knot or loop, no mouth ever stops our exchanges. Between us the house has no wall, the clearing no enclosure, language no circularity. When you kiss me, the world grows so large that the horizon itself disappears. Are we unsatisfied? Yes, if that means we are never finished. If our pleasure consists in moving, being moved, endlessly. Always in motion: openness is never spent nor sated.

We haven't been taught, nor allowed, to express multiplicity. To do that is to speak improperly. Of course, we might—we were supposed to?—exhibit one "truth" while sensing, withholding, muffling another. Truth's other side—its complement? its remainder?—stayed hidden. Secret. Inside and outside, we were not supposed to be the same. That doesn't suit their desires. Veiling and unveiling: isn't that what interests them? What keeps them busy? Always repeating the same operation, every time. On every woman.

You/I become two, then, for their pleasure. But thus divided in two, one outside, the other inside, you no longer embrace yourself, or me. Outside, you try to conform to an alien order. Exiled from yourself, you fuse with everything you meet. You imitate whatever comes close. You become whatever touches you. In your eagerness to find yourself again, you move indefinitely far from yourself. From me. Taking one model after another, passing from master to master, changing face, form, and language with each new power that dominates you. You/we are sundered; as you allow yourself to be abused, you become an impassive travesty. You no longer return indifferent; you return closed, impenetrable.

Speak to me. You can't? You no longer want to? You want to hold back? Remain silent? White? Virginal? Keep the inside self to yourself? But it doesn't exist without the other. Don't tear yourself apart like that with choices imposed on you. *Between us,* there's no rupture between virginal and nonvirginal. No event that makes us women. Long before your birth, you touched yourself, innocently. Your/my body doesn't acquire its sex through an operation. Through the action of some power, function, or organ. Without any intervention or special manipulation, you are a woman already. There is no need for an outside; the other already affects you. It is inseparable from you. You are altered forever, through and through. That is your crime, which you didn't commit: you disturb their love of property.

How can I tell you that there is no possible evil in your sexual pleasure—you who are a stranger to good(s). That the fault only comes about when they strip you of your openness and close you up, marking you with signs of possession; then they can break in, commit infractions and transgressions and play other games with the law. Games in which they—and you?—speculate on your whiteness. If we play along, we let ourselves be abused, destroyed. We remain indefinitely distant from ourselves to support the pursuit of their ends. That would be our flaw. If we submit to their reasoning, we are guilty. Their strategy, intentional or not, is calculated to make us guilty.

You come back, divided: "we" are no more. You are split into red and white, black and white: how can we find each other again? How can we touch each other once more? Cut up, dispatched, finished: our pleasure is trapped in their system, where a virgin is one as yet unmarked by them, for them. One who is not yet made woman by and for them. Not yet imprinted with their sex, their language. Not yet penetrated, possessed by them. Remaining in that candor that waits for them, that is nothing without them, a void without them. A virgin is the future of their exchanges, transactions, transports. A kind of reserve for their explorations, consummations, exploitations. The advent of their desire, Not of ours.

How can I say it? That we are women from the start. That we don't have to be turned into women by them, labeled by them, made holy and profaned by them. That that has always already happened, without their efforts. And that their history, their stories, constitute the locus of our displacement. It's not that we have a territory of our own; but their fatherland, family, home, discourse, imprison us in enclosed spaces where we cannot keep on moving, living, as ourselves. Their properties are our exile. Their enclosures, the death of our love. Their words, the gag upon our lips.

How can we speak so as to escape from their compartments, their schemas, their distinctions and oppositions: virginal/deflowered, pure/impure, innocent/experienced . . . How can we shake off the chain of these terms, free ourselves from their categories, rid ourselves of their names? Disengage ourselves, *alive,* from their concepts? Without reserve, without the immaculate whiteness that shores up their systems. You know that we are never completed, but that we only embrace ourselves whole. That one after another, parts—of the body, of space, of time—interrupt the flow of our blood. Paralyze, petrify, immobilize us. Make us paler. Almost frigid.

Wait. My blood is coming back. From their senses. It's warm inside us again. Among us. Their words are emptying out, becoming bloodless, Dead skins. While our lips are growing red again. They're stirring, moving, they want to speak. You mean . . .? What? Nothing. Everything. Yes. Be patient. You'll say it all. Begin with what you feel, right here, right now. Our all will come.

But you can't anticipate it, foresee it, program it. Our all cannot be projected, or mastered. Our whole body is moved.

No surface holds. No figure, line, or point remains. No ground subsists. But no abyss, either. Depth, for us, is not a chasm. Without a solid crust, there is no precipice. Our depth is the thickness of our body, our all touching itself. Where top and bottom, inside and outside, in front and behind, above and below are not separated, remote, out of touch. Our all intermingled. Without breaks or gaps.

If you/I hesitate to speak, isn't it because we are afraid of not speaking well? But what is "well" or "badly"? With what are we conforming if we speak "well"? What hierarchy, what subordination lurks there, waiting to break our resistance? What claim to raise ourselves up in a worthier discourse? Erection is no business of ours: we are at home on the flatlands. We have so much space to share. Our horizon will never stop expanding; we are always open. Stretching out, never ceasing to unfold ourselves, we have so many voices to invent in order to express all of us everywhere, even in our gaps, that all the time there is will not be enough. We can never complete the circuit, explore our periphery: we have so many dimensions. If you want to speak "well," you pull yourself in, you become narrower as you rise. Stretching upward, reaching higher, you pull yourself away from the limitless realm of your body. Don't make yourself erect, you'll leave us. The sky isn't up there: it's between us.

And don't worry about the "right" word. There isn't any. No truth between our lips. There is room enough for everything to exist. Everything is worth exchanging, nothing is privileged, nothing is refused. Exchange? Everything is exchanged, yet there are no transactions. Between us, there are no proprietors, no purchasers, no determinable objects, no prices. Our bodies are nourished by our mutual pleasure. Our abundance is inexhaustible: it knows neither want nor plenty. Since we give each other (our) all, with nothing held back, nothing hoarded, our exchanges are without terms, without end. How can I say it? The language we know is so limited . . .

Why speak? you'll ask me. We feel the same things at the same time. Aren't my hands, my eyes, my mouth, my lips, my body enough for you? Isn't what they are saying to you sufficient? I could answer "yes," but that would be too easy. Too much a matter of reassuring you/us.

If we don't invent a language, if we don't find our body's language, it will have too few gestures to accompany our story. We shall tire of the same ones, and leave our desires unexpressed, unrealized. Asleep again, unsatisfied, we shall fall back upon the words of men—who, for their part, have "known" for a long time. But *not our body*. Seduced, attracted, fascinated, ecstatic with our becoming, we shall remain paralyzed. Deprived of *our movements*. Rigid, whereas we are made for endless change. Without leaps or falls, and without repetition.

Keep on going, without getting out of breath. Your body is not the same today as yesterday. Your body remembers. There's no need for *you* to remember. No need to hold fast to yesterday, to store it up as capital in your head. Your memory? Your body expresses yesterday in what it wants today. If you think: yesterday I was, tomorrow I shall be, you are thinking: I have died a little. Be what you are becoming, without clinging to what you might have been, what you might yet be. Never settle. Let's leave definitiveness to the undecided; we don't need it. Our body, right here, right now, gives us a very different certainty. Truth is necessary for those who are so distanced from their body that they have forgotten it. But their "truth" immobilizes us, turns us into statues, if we can't loose its hold on us. If we can't defuse its power by trying to say, right here and now, how we are moved.

You are moving. You never stay still. You never stay. You never "are." How can I say "you," when you are always other?

How can I speak to you? You remain in flux, never congealing or solidifying. What will make that current flow into words? It is multiple, devoid of causes, meanings, simple qualities. Yet it cannot be decomposed. These movements cannot be described as the passage from a beginning to an end. These rivers flow into no single, definitive sea. These streams are without fixed banks, this body without fixed boundaries. This unceasing mobility. This life—which will perhaps be called our restlessness, whims, pretenses, or lies. All this remains very strange to anyone claiming to stand on solid ground.

Speak, all the same. Between us, "hardness" isn't necessary. We know the contours of our bodies well enough to love fluidity. Our density can do without trenchancy or rigidity. We are not drawn to dead bodies.

But how can we stay alive when we are far apart? There's the danger. How can I wait for you to return if when you're far away from me you cannot also be near? If I have nothing palpable to help me recall in the here and now the touch of our bodies. Open to the infinity of our separation, wrapped up in the intangible sensation of absence, how can we continue to live as ourselves? How can we keep ourselves from becoming absorbed once again in their violating language? From being embodied as mourning. We must learn to speak to each other so that we can embrace from afar. When I touch myself, I am surely remembering you. But so much has been said, and said of us, that separates us.

Let's hurry and invent our own phrases. So that everywhere and always we can continue to embrace. We are so subtle that nothing can stand in our way, nothing can stop us from reaching each other, even fleetingly, if we can find means of communication that have *our* density. We shall pass imperceptibly through every barrier, unharmed, to find each other. No one will see a thing. Our strength lies in the very weakness of our resistance. For a long time now they have appreciated what our suppleness is worth for their own embraces and impressions. Why not enjoy it ourselves? Rather than letting ourselves be subjected to their branding. Rather than being fixed, stabilized, immobilized. Separated.

Don't cry. One day we'll manage to say ourselves. And what we say will be even lovelier than our tears. Wholly fluent.

Already, I carry you with me everywhere. Not like a child, a burden, a weight, however beloved and precious. You are not *in me*. I do not contain you or retain you in my stomach, my arms, my head. Nor in my memory, my mind, my language. You are there, like my skin. With you I am certain of existing beyond all appearances, all disguises, all designations. I am assured of living because you are duplicating my life. Which doesn't mean that you give me yours, or subordinate it to mine. The fact that you live lets me know I am alive, so long as you are neither my counterpart nor my copy.

How can I say it differently? We exist only as two? We live by twos beyond all mirages, images, and mirrors. Between us, one is not the "real" and the other her imitation; one is not the original and the other her copy. Although we can dissimulate perfectly within their economy, we relate to one another without simulacrum. Our resemblance does without semblances: for in our bodies, we are already the same. Touch yourself, touch me, you'll "see."

No need to fashion a mirror image to be "doubled," to repeat ourselves—a second time. Prior to any representation, we are two. Let those two—made for you by your blood, evoked for you by my body—come together alive. You will always have the touching beauty of a first time, if you aren't congealed in reproductions. You will always be moved for the first time, if you aren't immobilized in any form of repetition.

We can do without models, standards, or examples. Let's never give ourselves orders, commands, or prohibitions. Let our imperatives be only appeals to move, to be moved, together. Let's never lay down the law to each other, or moralize, or make war. Let's not claim to be right, or claim the right to criticize one another. If one of us sits in judgment, our existence comes to an end. And what I love in you, in myself, in us no longer takes place: the birth that is never accomplished, the body never created once and for all, the form never definitively completed, the face always still to be formed. The lips never opened or closed on a truth.

Light, for us, is not violent. Not deadly. For us the sun does not simply rise or set. Day and night are mingled in our gazes. Our gestures. Our bodies. Strictly speaking, we cast no shadow. There is no danger that one or the other may be a darker double. I want to remain nocturnal, and find my night softly luminous, in you. And don't by any means imagine that I love you shining like a beacon, lording it over everything around you. If we divide light from night, we give up the lightness of our mixture, solidify those heterogeneities that make us so consistently whole. We put ourselves into watertight compartments, break ourselves up into parts, cut ourselves in two, and more. Whereas we are always one and the other, at the same time. If we separate ourselves that way, we "all" stop being born. Without limits or borders, except those of our moving bodies.

And only the limiting effect of time can make us stop speaking to each other. Don't worry. I—continue. Under all these artificial constraints of time and space, I embrace you endlessly. Others may make fetishes of us to separate us: that's their business. Let's not immobilize ourselves in these borrowed notions.

And if I have so often insisted on negatives: *not, nor, without* . . . it has been to remind you, to remind us, that we only touch each other naked. And that, to find ourselves once again in that state, we have a lot to take off. So many representations, so many appearances separate us from each other. They have wrapped us for so long in their desires, we have adorned ourselves so often to please them, that we have come to forget the feel of our own skin. Removed from our skin, we remain distant. You and I, apart.

You? I? That's still saying too much. Dividing too sharply between us: all.

Publisher's Note and Notes on Selected Terms

Publisher's Note

Some modifications of the format of the original edition of this book have been made for the convenience of readers and some in accordance with the conventions of book-making in the English-speaking world.

Notes on Selected Terms

"Alice" underground (*"Alice" sous-terre*)
In the original, Irigaray rewrites the name Soutter (the director of the film that is the ostensible subject of "The Looking-Glass, from the Other Side") to point up the subversive or underground nature of her speaker's perspective, that of a female subject who refuses to be circumscribed or named according to the rules of patriarchal logic.

all (*toute[s]*)
In translation, it is not always possible to convey Irigaray's idiosyncratic transformations of French grammatical structures, as in *toute(s)*, a female subject that is simultaneously singular and plural, as such, an example of her "speaking (as) woman" (*parler-femme*).

commodities (*marchandises*)
Because English lacks gender, the term is neutralized in translation,

and Irigaray's emphasis on the commodity as feminine or female matter cannot be fully translated. Thus, ironically, her larger point—that the organization of sexual difference is reflected in language as well as in social practices—is slightly blunted due to the differences between actual languages.

"dragonfly" (*"Libellule"*)
The name of the cap that is passed around in the film discussed in "The Looking-Glass, from the Other Side."

ek-sistance (*ek-sistance*)
Existence as conscious separation or differentiation from nature: the state of being opposite to that generally ascribed to the feminine.

indifferent (*indifférente[s]*)

a) Within the masculine order, the woman is indifferent in the sense of non-different or undifferentiated because she has no right to her own sexual difference but must accept masculine definitions and appropriations of it.
b) As a consequence, she is indifferent in the sense of detached or remote because of the imposture of her position.
c) From a feminine perspective, however, she might experience difference differently, in relation to her resemblance to another woman rather than to a masculine standard. (V. "When Our Lips Speak Together.")

masquerade (*la mascarade*)
An alienated or false version of femininity arising from the woman's awareness of the man's desire for her to be his other, the masquerade permits woman to experience desire not in her own right but as the man's desire situates her.

mimicry (*mimétisme*)
An interim strategy for dealing with the realm of discourse (where the speaking subject is posited as masculine), in which the woman deliberately assumes the feminine style and posture assigned to her within this discourse in order to uncover the mechanisms by which it exploits her.

one, oneness (*le un*)

The universal standard and privileged form in our systems of representation, *oneness* expresses the requirements for unitary representations of signification and identity. Within such a system, in which the masculine standard takes itself as a universal, it would be impossible to represent the duality or plurality of the female sex and of a possible language in analogy with it.

other/same (*autre/même*)

A related tendency in Western discourse which privileges masculine "sameness-unto-itself" as the basis of signification and identity and, as a consequence, posits the feminine as other only in relation to masculine sameness, that is, not as a different mode of signification.

proper, proper name, property, appropriate (*propre, nom propre, propriété, approprier*)

This word cluster suggests close connections between the related systems of capitalism and patriarchy—more specifically, between their demands for order, neatness, the proper name, and the proper or literal meaning of a word, on the one hand, and the concepts of property ownership and appropriation, on the other.

questions (*questions*)

A habitual mode in Irigaray's writing, because it introduces a plurality of voices and facilitates the examination of a priori concepts without, however, insisting upon definitive answers or revisions of the systems of thought that are brought into question.

retraversal (*retraversée*)

The process of going back through social, intellectual, and linguistic practices to reexamine and unravel their conceptual bases, in analogy with Alice's voyages of exploration in *Through the Looking-Glass*.

reversal (*renversement*)

A reversal in the hierarchies of power, so that the formerly "inferior" term then occupies the position of the "superior" term but without altering the nature of their relations.

self-affection, self-touching (*auto-affection, se retoucher*)
A mode of signification in analogy with the openness and plurality of female sexuality (which is always auto-erotically in touch with itself) as opposed to the closed or singular mode of phallic discourse.

speaking (as) woman (*parler-femme*)
Not so much a definitive method as an experimental process or a discovery of the possible connections between female sexuality and writing, "speaking (as) woman" would try to disrupt or alter the syntax of discursive logic, based on the requirements of univocity and masculine sameness, in order to express the plurality and mutuality of feminine difference and mime the relations of "self-affection."

standard (*étalon*)
The masculine as the standard of value, in relation to which the feminine acquires significance and worth. The resonance of *étalon,* which also means *stallion,* is, however, lost in translation, as is the sense of *étalonnage* as not only a standardization but also a kind of stud-service that divides the socio-sexual order into what Irigaray calls masculine "producer-subjects" and feminine "commodity-objects."

Library of Congress Cataloging in Publication Data
Irigaray, Luce.
This sex which is not one.
Translation of: Ce sexe qui n'en est pas un.
1. Women—Psychology. 2. Women and psychoanalysis.
3. Feminity (Philosophy) 4. Sex (Psychology)
I. Title.
HQ1206.I713 1985 155.3'333 84-23013
ISBN 0-8014-1546-2 (alk. paper)
ISBN 0-8014-9331-5 (pbk.: alk. paper)